Tax DOs and DON'Ts for Property Companies

By

Lee Sharpe

Publisher Details
This guide is published by Tax Portal Ltd. 3 Sanderson Close, Great Sankey, Warrington, Cheshire, WA5 3LN.

'Tax DOs and DON'Ts for Property Companies – First published in May 2008, Second Edition May 2009. Third Edition August 2010. Fourth Edition May 2011. Fifth Edition April 2012. Sixth Edition May 2013. Seventh Edition April 2014. Eighth Edition April 2015. Ninth Edition April 2016. Tenth Edition April 2017 Eleventh Edition April 2018. Twelfth Edition March 2019. Thirteenth Edition May 2020. Fourteenth Edition April 2021. Fifteenth Edition April 2022. Sixteenth Edition April 2023. Seventeenth Edition June 2024.

Copyright
The right of Lee Sharpe and Tax Portal Ltd to be identified as the authors of this guide has been asserted in accordance with the Copyright, Designs and Patents Act 1988, England.

© 2009-2024 Lee Sharpe and Tax Portal Ltd.

A CIP Copy of this book is available from the British Library.

978-1-7394153-7-2

All rights reserved
All rights reserved. No part of this guide may be reproduced or transmitted in any form or by any means, electronically or mechanically, including photocopying, recording or any information storage or retrieval system, without prior permission in writing from the publisher.

Permission is granted to print a single hardcopy version of this guide for your personal use only.

Trademarks
Property Tax Portal, Tax Portal Ltd and other Tax Portal Ltd services/products referenced in this guide are registered trademarks or trademarks of Tax Portal Ltd in the UK and/or other countries.

Disclaimer

a) This guide is produced for General guidance only, and professional advice should be sought before any decision is made. Individual circumstances can vary and therefore no responsibility can be accepted by the author, Lee Sharpe, or the publisher Tax Portal Ltd, for any action taken, or any decision made to refrain from action, by any readers of this guide.

b) Tax rules and legislation are constantly changing and therefore the information printed in this guide is correct at the time of printing – June 2024.

c) Neither the author nor Tax Portal Ltd offer financial, legal or investment advice. If you require such advice, then we urge you to seek the opinion of an appropriate professional in the relevant field. We care about your success and therefore encourage you to take appropriate advice before you put any of your financial or other resources at risk. Don't forget, investment values can decrease as well as increase.

d) To the fullest extent permitted by law, Lee Sharpe and Tax Portal Ltd do not accept liability for any direct, indirect, special, consequential or other losses or damages of whatsoever kind arising from using this guide.

The guide itself is provided 'as is' without express or implied warranty.

e) Lee Sharpe and Tax Portal Ltd reserve the right to alter any part of this guide at any time without notice.

Contents

About Lee Sharpe 9

1. **About This Guide** 10
   1.1. *Background and Rough Chronology* 10
   1.2. *Tax Rates and Devolved Taxes* 14
   1.3. *Stamp Taxes* 14

2. **Choosing the Right Structure** 18
   2.1. *The Basics: Sole Trader – "One Man Band"* 18
   2.2. *The Basics: Partnership* 18
   2.3. *The Basics: Limited Company* 19
   2.4. *Types of Partnerships – or is it a Joint Venture?* 19
      2.4.1. A "Limited Partnership" 20
      2.4.2. A Limited Liability Partnership (also referred to as an "LLP") 20

3. **Getting to Grips with Limited Companies** 22
   3.1. *The Different Types of Limited Company* 22
   3.2. *The Basic Rules for a Company* 22

4. **Understanding Corporation Tax** 25
   4.1. *The Rates of Corporation Tax* 25
   4.2. *Associated Companies – Anti-Fragmenting Regime* 25
   4.3. *Key Dates for the Company* 27
   4.4. *Benefiting from the Favourable Company Taxes* 28
   4.5. *Extracting the Cash from the Company* 29
      4.5.1. Paying a Salary 29
      4.5.2. Paying Dividends Instead 31
      4.5.3. Paying Dividends and a Salary 34
      4.5.4. Are Dividends Always Better? 37
   4.6. *Beyond the Basics* 38

5. **Building Up a Property Portfolio Using a Company** 40
   5.1. *Using a Company to Grow Your Property Portfolio* 40

6. **Disallowance of Mortgage Interest on Residential Properties** 42

7. **Everything You Need to Know About Dividend Payments** 44
   7.1. *Working with "Distributable Profits"* 44
   7.2. *Who Gets the Dividends?* 45
   7.3. *The Two Types of Dividend* 46
      7.3.1. A "Final" Dividend 46

		7.3.2.	An "Interim" Dividend.	46
	7.4.		*Getting the Paperwork Right*	*46*
		7.4.1.	Sample – Meeting Minute	47
		7.4.2.	Sample – Dividend Confirmation	49
	7.5.		*Two Pitfalls to Avoid when Making Dividend Payments*	*50*
		7.5.1.	"Illegal" Dividends.	50
		7.5.2.	Timing of Dividends	50
	7.6.		*Using Dividend Waivers – An Effective Tax Planning Tool*	*50*
	7.7.		*Watch out for the "Settlements" Legislation*	*51*
8.	**The Property Development Company**			**53**
	8.1.		*The Property Developer*	*53*
	8.2.		*Companies and Property Developers*	*53*
	8.3.		*The Construction Industry Scheme ("CIS")*	*56*
	8.4.		*Other Considerations for Property Developers – and Occasional Developers*	*57*
9.	**Incorporation Relief(s)**			**60**
	9.1.		*Transferring Assets into Your Company*	*60*
		9.1.1.	Holdover Relief for Gifts of Business Assets	60
		9.1.2.	Incorporation in Exchange for Shares	62
	9.2.		*Watch Out for Some Pitfalls*	*63*
		9.2.1.	"Preordained Series of Transactions"	63
		9.2.2.	Stamp Duty Land Tax	64
		9.2.3.	What is a "Business"?	64
		9.2.4.	Highly-Geared Businesses	64
		9.2.5.	Shifting Values – IHT and CGT and Preserving Symmetry	64
	9.3.		*Comparing Incorporation and Gift Relief – Key Points*	*66*
	9.4.		*Incorporating an Existing Property Investment Portfolio*	*66*
	9.5.		*Disincorporation – an Overview of the Tax Aspects*	*67*
10.	**Entrepreneurs' Relief ("ER") from CGT – Now "Business Asset Disposal Relief" – and Investors' Relief**			**69**
11.	**Reinvestment Relief**			**71**
	11.1.		*Property Investors and Reinvestment Relief*	*71*
		11.1.1.	Business Assets	71
		11.1.2.	Furnished Holiday Lettings	71
		11.1.3.	Reinvestment Relief - Example	72
	11.2.		*Deferring Capital Gains by Reinvesting*	*73*
		11.2.1.	Enterprise Investment Scheme (EIS)	73
12.	**Some Property Tax Pitfalls**			**76**
	12.1.		*Partnerships?*	*76*
		12.1.1.	Why Does It Matter?	76
	12.2.		*SDLT Implications of Transfers Involving A Mortgage*	*78*
	12.3.		*SDLT, Partnerships And Incorporation*	*79*
	12.4.		*Increased SDLT Risk For Companies – Indecision Costs Money!*	*80*

12.5.	Annual Tax On "Enveloped Dwellings" (ATED)	81
12.6.	Foreign Ownership	82
12.6.1.	UK Capital Gains by Non-Residents	82
12.6.2.	SDLT Surcharge for Non-Resident Investors	84
12.7.	International Tax Co-Operation	84
12.8.	Using Companies for Specific Development Opportunities: Profits from Dealing In or Developing UK Land ("Transactions in Land")	85
12.9.	How Limited is Your Limited Liability?	89

13. Close Companies 92

13.1.	What is a Close Company?	92
13.2.	Special Rules for Close Companies	93
13.3.	The Meaning of a "Distribution" From a Close Company	93
13.4.	Loan To Participator – "s455 Tax"	93
13.5.	Beware Close Investment Holding Companies & "Properties Let Commercially"	96

14. The Directors' Tax Liabilities 98

14.1.	Tax on Non-Cash Benefits	98
14.2.	Expenses	98
14.2.1.	Travelling expenses	98
14.2.2.	Cars	99
14.2.3.	Using Your Own Car for Business	99
14.2.4.	Using Cars for Sole Traders and Partnerships	99
14.2.5.	Three Important Differences to Remember	99
14.3.	Other Expenses	100
14.4.	Shares as Rewards	101
14.5.	FIVE Tax Free Benefits	102

15. Companies and Tax Investigations 105

15.1.	"Aspect" Enquiries	105
15.2.	"Compliance" Enquiries	105
15.3.	Full Enquiry	106
15.4.	"Grossing up"	106
15.5.	Company Investigation Settlements	108
15.6.	Be Careful what the Inspector "Presumes"	110
15.7.	Watch Out for the Contractual Disclosure Facility (CDF) and COP 9	111
15.8.	Four Golden Rules of Tax Investigations	111

16. Getting Your Exit Strategy Right 112

16.1.	Everybody Has an Exit Strategy	112
16.2.	The THREE Most Common Exit Strategies	112
16.3.	Selling the Business	112
16.3.1.	Benefits of Buying the Shares in the Company	112
16.3.2.	Drawbacks of Buying the Shares in the Company	113
16.3.3.	Benefits of Selling the Shares in the Company	113

- 16.3.4. Benefits of Selling the Company's Assets and then Liquidating 114
- 16.4. *Selling the Company's Shares* 114
  - 16.4.1. "Earn-outs" 114
  - 16.4.2. "Employment-Related Shares or Securities" 116
  - 16.4.3. Payments Under Warranties and Indemnities 116
  - 16.4.4. "Compensation for Loss of Office" 116
  - 16.4.5. Pre-Sale Tax Planning 116
  - 16.4.6. Company Purchase of Own Shares 117
  - 16.4.7. Timing 117
  - 16.4.8. Gifts to Spouse / Civil Partner 118
  - 16.4.9. Substantial Shareholding Exemption 118
  - 16.4.10. Post-Sale Tax Planning 119
  - 16.4.11. Tax Shelters 119
  - 16.4.12. Losses 119
- 16.5. *Sales of Assets and Liquidation of Company* 119
- 16.6. *How to Liquidate a Company* 120
  - 16.6.1. A Formal Liquidation 120
  - 16.6.2. An Informal Liquidation 120
  - 16.6.3. But Beware "Phoenix Arrangements" 120
- 16.7. *Dying in Harness and/or Living Off the Profits* 122

17. Inheritance Tax and Companies 124

- 17.1. *IHT – the Basics* 124
- 17.2. *Nil Rate Band (NRB)* 124
- 17.3. *Residence Nil Rate Band (RNRB)* 125
- 17.4. *PETs* 126
- 17.5. *Gift with Reservation of Benefit* 127
- 17.6. *Spouse Exemption* 128
- 17.7. *Business Property Relief* 128
- 17.8. *Close Companies and IHT* 129

18. Finding an Accountant 132

- 18.1. *Accountancy Qualifications* 132
- 18.2. *General Advisor or Tax Specialist?* 133
- 18.3. *How to Choose Your Adviser* 133
  - 18.3.1. Will I Need a Tax Adviser or an Accountant? 133
  - 18.3.2. What Qualifications? 133
  - 18.3.3. How Much Experience do they Have? 134
  - 18.3.4. How Much Will It Cost? 134
  - 18.3.5. Professional Bodies 134
  - 18.3.6. What About Indemnity Cover? 134
  - 18.3.7. How do I Contact My Tax Adviser / Accountant? 135
  - 18.3.8. Keep up to Date with Tax Legislation Changes 135
  - 18.3.9. What if I Have an Emergency? 136
  - 18.3.10. Does the Adviser Sell 'Off the Shelf' Packages? 136

19. The Importance of Tax Planning 137

- 19.1. *Knowing When to Consider Planning* 137
  - 19.1.1. Buying 137
  - 19.1.2. Repairs and Refurbishment 138

	19.1.3.	Selling	138
	19.1.4.	Life changes	139
	19.1.5.	Politics	139
	19.1.6.	End and Start of Tax Year	139
19.2.	*The Real Benefits of Tax Planning*		*140*
	19.2.1.	Paying Less Tax	140
	19.2.2.	Clear 'Entrance' and 'Exit' Strategies	140
	19.2.3.	Staying Focused	140
	19.2.4.	Improving Cash Flow	140
	19.2.5.	Avoiding Common Tax Traps	141
19.3.	*The Golden Tax Rules*		*141*
	19.3.1.	Education…Education…Education	141
	19.3.2.	Prevention is Better Than Cure	141

20. Appendix A – Template Documents 143

21. Appendix B – Tables 146

21.1.	*Comparing Individual Property Investor with a Company (2023/24 v 2024/25)*	*147*
21.2.	*Comparing Individual Property Investor with a Company (2024/25; differing interest costs)*	*150*
21.3.	*Comparing Individual Property Investor with a Company (2015/16 v 2024/25 "No Interest")*	*152*
21.4.	*Comparing Net Property Developer (Trading) Income: Personal v Through a Company (2023/24 v 2024/25)*	*154*
21.5.	*Comparing Net Property Developer (Trading) Income: Personal v Through a Company (2015/16 v 2024/25)*	*157*

About Lee Sharpe

Lee is a Chartered Tax Adviser and tax consultant with over twenty years' experience in helping individuals, families, businesses and advisers with their tax affairs.

Lee writes extensively on tax matters for taxpayers and their advisers, including through the Tax Insider publications, Bloomsbury Professional and the TaxationWeb website. He also lectures taxpayers, accountants and other financial advisers on tax issues.

While he has appeared on TV to comment on tax matters, it was only long enough to establish that he really has a face for radio, and to give fellow members of his local CIOT branch sufficient ammunition with which to embarrass him at committee meetings.

When he is not giving tax advice or writing about tax matters, he is busy looking after his two children – not because he likes them, but because he wants to make sure that his office is not used exclusively for business purposes...

1. About This Guide

One of the most common questions tax advisers often get asked is "should I use a limited company for this business, or not?"

There is no simple answer to this question, and there is a great deal of myth and misunderstanding about limited companies.

The purpose of this guide is to set out the benefits and drawbacks of using a limited company as a vehicle for a property business, and to compare them with other possible business structures. This guide assumes you have no previous knowledge or experience of limited companies. By the time you finish it, we hope you will have a much clearer idea of the way a company works, and whether it is the right vehicle for your business, and what you hope to achieve.

1.1. Background and Rough Chronology

Broadly over the last couple of decades, there has been pressure on many small businesses to *incorporate* (i.e., for people to transfer their business into a limited company), as exemplified by the tax breaks introduced by the Chancellor of the Exchequer in 2000 and in 2002, that were potentially very attractive – a strong "pull effect". These tax breaks were withdrawn from April 2006, following which, the decision whether to incorporate or not has become an increasingly fine one to gauge.

More recently, the 2015 Summer Budget heralded a significant increase in the effective rates of dividend taxation, such that company dividends (and perhaps even incorporation itself) lost some of their shine. But the Chancellor also announced tax relief restrictions for Buy-to-Let landlords operating as individuals (whether solely, in joint names or in partnership) that left companies largely unaffected. In large swathes of the residential letting market, the race is very much back on, given how punitive those interest relief restrictions can be in practice a "push effect".

The 2021 March Budget announced that Corporation Tax rates would be increased back to a "main" rate of 25% (where 'profits' exceed £250,000), broadly as follows:

- Profits up to £50,000   19.0% (new "Small Profits Rate" – but also previously the Main Rate since 2017)
- Profits £50,001 - £250,000   26.5% (new "Marginal Rate")
- Profits £250,001 and above   25.0% (higher "Main Rate")

Strictly, the main rate has been increased, while new Small and Marginal Rate bands have been squeezed in to apply to lower profit levels (FA 2021 s 7, Sch 1).

This stepped hike in Corporation Tax rates has also revived the anti-avoidance regime for "associated" (broadly, connected) companies, much to the delight of older/more experienced tax practitioners like me, who remember how much fun it was first time around – see 4.2

Readers may recall that it was only a few years ago, that one of Mr. Sunak's predecessors justified the "reform" of (i.e., significant increase to) dividend taxation rates as being necessary in order to compensate for enjoying lower Corporation Tax rates. Alas, it seems Mr. Sunak may have "missed that memo", since his reversal of Corporation Tax rates back *up* to 25% appears to omit any corresponding reduction in dividend taxation. To put it another way, many small company owners will find their Corporation Tax bills rising, ostensibly to help pay for government pandemic assistance that they didn't actually get.

Note that the 2021 Budget did **not** say that the increased Corporation Tax rate from 1 April 2023 was intended to be a temporary measure, despite Mr. Kwarteng's best(?) attempts in September 2022, most of what the then-Chancellor Kwarteng said about changing the direction of UK taxation policy has since been discarded – much like the Chancellor himself – as an abortive nightmare episode, whose only lasting legacy is a significant rise in interest rates. So, after a brief wobble, Corporation Tax rates are increasing as planned.

Broadly since the 2023 Spring Budget, (inclusive), we have also had the following announcements that are of particular relevance to property taxation and companies:

Income Tax –

- In the 2023 Spring Budget, the zero-rate so-called "Dividend Allowance" for Income Tax (it is in fact a nil-rate band) was cut from £2,000 to:
  - £1,000 for 2023/24, then
  - £500 from 2024/25 onwards

- Additional Rate Threshold lowered to £125,400 – while the oft-stated aim of reducing the main Basic Rate of Income Tax from 20/% to 19% seems further away than ever, we *have* had a reduction in the threshold at which the Additional Rate of 45% becomes payable: it used to apply once adjusted incomes exceeded £150,000 but applies starting at £125,140 from 2023/24 onwards (the threshold is set precisely, so that it takes effect immediately that the individual's adjusted income exceeds the point at which the Personal Allowance is completely forfeit). By reducing the point on the income scale at which a higher rate of tax is payable, this measure will of course increase tax revenues to the Crown (November 2022 Fiscal Statement).

- The standard personal pension Annual Allowance was increased from £40,000 to £60,000 per year, from April 2023; the cumulative Lifetime Allowance charge is also abolished from April 2023, while the Lifetime Allowance itself was withdrawn from April 2024, under Chancellor Kwarteng's September 2022 "Growth Plan".

National Insurance Contributions (NICs) –

- Autumn Statement November 2023 announced:
  - Employees' Class 1 Primary Contributions were reduced from 12% to 10% with effect from 6 January 2024 (i.e., in the middle of the 2023/24 tax year) and
  - Self-Employed Class 4 NICs were to be reduced from 9% to 8% from 6 April 2024 (i.e., for 2024/25 onwards)

- Spring Budget in March 2024 further announced that:
  - Employers' Class 1 Primary Contributions would be reduced from 10% to just 8% from 6 April 2024 and
  - Self-Employed Class 4 NICs would be reduced to just 6% from 6 April 2024

- Furthermore, the self-employed Class 2 NICs, that "earn" entitlement to State Pension, would *effectively* be chargeable at £Nil for anyone with self-employed profits of £6,725pa and upwards – while still "earning" their contribution year for State Pension purposes; however, individuals with profits below £6,725pa in the tax year could choose to secure their annual credit for State Pension purposes by making a **voluntary** contribution of £3.45per week x 52 = £179.40 in Class 2 contributions.

- and the Government stated in March 2024 that it intends ultimately to abolish NICs altogether (although it is difficult to see how this might be achieved without raising Income Taxes, unless the Government also intends to abolish some of the benefits that NICs nominally fund)

Capital Gains Tax (CGT) –

- In the 2023 Spring Budget, the Capital Gains Tax Annual Exemption was reduced for individuals, from £12,300 to:
    - £6,000 for 2023/24, then
    - £3,000 from 2024/25 onwards

- The 2024 Spring Budget included that the CGT higher rate for disposals of residential property was reduced, for disposals on or after 6 April 2024, from 28% to 24%.

Stamp Duty Land Tax (England & Northern Ireland) –

An increase to the initial nil rate band of Stamp Duty Land Tax from the standard first £125,000 of consideration to £250,000, (even for property businesses), was announced as a permanent change in the September 2023 "Growth Plan", but was down-graded to just a temporary measure, ending 31 March 2025, in the March 2023 Budget (see also 1.3 below).

Spring Budget 2024 announced that Stamp Duty Land Tax Multiple Dwellings Relief would be abolished for transactions with an effective date 1 June 2024 and onwards (with savings for 'old' contracts entered into prior to Budget Day 6 March 2024, etc.)

Furnished Holiday Accommodation (aka "Furnished Holiday Lettings") –

The Spring Budget 2024 also included the announcement that the "Furnished Holiday Letting Regime" was to be abolished from 6 April 2025 **(although it remains to be seen whether or not this will be affected by the General Election)**

Capital Allowances –

Long-standing 100% Annual Investment Allowance (AIA) rate of £1million pa formally put on a permanent footing, as announced on 23 September 2022 in Chancellor Kwarteng's "Growth Plan".

To the extent that bigger companies need more than £1million pa (for example, where the AIA has to be spread across several companies in a group), then there is now a "Full Expensing" First Year Allowance of 100% for main rate-eligible items and 50% for special rate-eligible items. It was initially announced on a temporary basis in Spring Budget 2023 then made permanent by the Autumn Statement in November 2023. But note that:

- It is available only to companies (unlike AIA, that is available also to individuals, and to partnerships composed entirely of individuals – no corporate members)

- Only for eligible plant and machinery that is new and unused – and not for cars (although vans may qualify; AIA is available on second hand goods)

- There is a special Clawback at 100%/50% of disposal proceeds that is taxable separately, (rather than simply being deducted from the corresponding pool as normal*) so a reasonably strong penalty for disposing of the assets while they still retain significant penalty

- *note that the *balancing* or *remaining* 50% of the proceeds on a special rate-qualifying asset's disposal will still be deducted from the special rate pool value, as normal

- Initially, it does **not** apply to assets acquired in order to be leased out (although the Chancellor said the regime would be extended to cover leased assets as soon as conditions allowed)

- But it does nevertheless apply to new assets bought to be fixed to property for letting (i.e., to "fixtures")

In general terms the new combination of higher Corporation Tax and dividend Income Tax rates may well prompt many director/shareholders of existing small or family-sized companies to question whether a company format remains appropriate, from an annual incomes tax perspective – particularly in those circumstances where they are highly profitable, and have to withdraw most of their annual profits for personal use every year.

Certainly, the comparison between unincorporated, self-employed businesses and their limited company counterparts has become much finer, and more nuanced. Some landlords – particularly those 'enjoying' substantial residential letting finance costs – have been spared this conundrum, thanks largely to the fact that the restriction of Income Tax relief on mortgage interest for unincorporated businesses is *so* expensive an alternative for them, that a mere 6% hike in Corporation Tax might make comparatively little difference. However, most landlords will fall between those two states, so further consideration is still in order. Interest costs may fluctuate, and mortgages may eventually be paid off.

For more consideration of the interaction between some of these changes over time, please see Appendix B, with tables comparing the effects over the years / for various profit levels.

But note also that there are other aspects to running a business through a limited company, and we shall in turn consider different scenarios that favour the company model, including:

- Re-cycling profits within the company to maximise tax-efficient "organic" growth (see Chapter 5)

- Running specific development projects within a company wrapper to maximise CGT relief (See 12.8)

- Deferring tax to a more suitable low-tax period (see Case Study 36)

Strictly speaking, there will now be scenarios where dividends are **not** more tax-efficient than salary or bonus payments, because the director's earnings will typically be deductible from business profits, and so save Corporation Tax, to such an extent (at such a rate) that the net income is marginally superior to taking a dividend from post-Corporation Tax profits. But these scenarios are relatively unusual so we have broadly continued to assume that director/shareholders will prefer dividends to salary, when modelling examples and comparisons in this book.

1.2. Tax Rates and Devolved Taxes

Unless otherwise indicated, we shall be using 2024/25 rates and allowances. 2017/18 saw the first tangible divergence in Scottish Income Tax rates when compared to the rest of the UK: for non-savings income; 2024/25 will continue a reasonably significant differential when comparing Scotland with the rest of the UK, as the Scottish government has moved not just thresholds but has introduced entirely new bands, and rates (although the differences in terms of outcomes – the amounts actually due – tend to be quite modest).

Strictly, 2019/20 was the first year of Welsh Income Tax rates. However, the National Assembly for Wales agreed to continue its alignment with "rest of UK" (i.e., non-Scottish) rates for the 2019/20 tax year and since – so far.

Interestingly for tax geeks, the Scottish and Welsh devolved taxing powers basically cannot affect savings income (including dividends) so that the Scottish and Welsh Higher Rate thresholds for bank interest, dividends and the like will be £50,270 in 2024/25, just like the rest of the UK – which potentially makes for some quirky calculations around the c£40,000 - c£50,000 income band for Scottish taxpayers, depending on the mix of incomes at that level. Note that "savings income" in this context does **not** include property income, which is subject to devolved taxes alongside earnings.

There are also potential knock-on implications, such as eligibility for the new Marriage Allowance. However, it should be emphasised that in very many cases, 'devolved' taxpayers will end up with similar results to rest-of-UK taxpayers and, even where they do not, the differences are likely to be relatively small. **This book will apply the 'standard' UK rates and thresholds throughout.**

1.3. Stamp Taxes

Stamp Duty Land Tax (SDLT) applies in England and Northern Ireland.

Land and Buildings Transaction Tax (LBTT) applies in Scotland.

Land Transactions Tax (LTT) applies in Wales.

While very similar, there *are* differences between the three regimes, and **readers operating in Scotland or Wales should get tax specific advice on LBTT and LTT respectively**; this guide follows the SDLT regime such as it applies in the rest of the UK.

The following tables apply only for residential property acquisitions.

Stamp Duty Land Tax (SDLT) – England and Northern Ireland

Purchase price, etc. – Residential Properties	SDLT Rate for purchases effective 23/09/22 to 31/03/25	SDLT Rate for purchases effective prior to 23/09/22	Higher Rate on Additional Dwellings (HRAD)*
Up to £125,000	0%	0%	+3%
The next £125,000 (the portion from £125,001 to £250,000)		2%	+3%
The next £675,000 (the portion from £250,001 to £925,000)	5%	5%	+3%
The next £575,000 (the portion from £925,001 to £1.5 million)	10%	10%	+3%
The remaining amount (the portion above £1.5 million)	12%	12%	+3%

*Companies cannot have a first "only or main home" so will pay the Higher Rate on Additional Dwellings extra 3% in practically all circumstances.

Note

i. Prior to 4 December 2014, SDLT used to be applied as a "slab" – i.e., a single rate applicable to the entire purchase price, rather than a "stepped" tax, as above. Strictly speaking, however, companies and other non-natural persons are still potentially liable to a 15% "slab rate" across the entire consideration, for single dwellings valued at more than £500,000, (effectively over-riding the above table), except where relief may be claimed. Having said that, the reliefs are quite widely applicable, and include property acquired for use in a property rental business, or development trade. We therefore assume that readers will be quite **unlikely** to have to contend with this special 15% "across the board" charge to SDLT (see also 12.4 below).

ii. There are discounted initial rates for "First-Time Buyers", and further supplements for "Non-Residents" acquiring interests in UK residential property – both as defined for the purposes of SDLT (see also 12.6.2 below).

Land and Buildings Transaction Tax (LBTT) – Scotland

Purchase price, etc. – Residential Properties	SDLT Rate for purchases effective 01/04/21	Additional Dwelling Supplement (ADS)*
Up to £145,000	0%	+6%

Purchase price, etc. – Residential Properties	SDLT Rate for purchases effective 01/04/21	Additional Dwelling Supplement (ADS)*
The next £105,000 (the portion from £145,001 to £250,000)	2%	+6%
The next £75,000 (the portion from £250,001 to £325,000)	5%	+6%
The next £425,000 (the portion from £325,001 to £750,000)	10%	+6%
The remaining amount (the portion above £750,000)	12%	+6%

*Note that the Scottish Additional Dwelling Supplement (broadly corresponding to the 3% Higher Rate for Additional Dwellings in England and Northern Ireland) increased from 4% to 6% of the purchase price, for contracts entered into on or after 16 December 2022.

Land Transaction Tax (LTT) - Wales

Purchase price, etc. – Residential Properties	LTT Rate for purchases effective 10/10/22 onwards	LTT Rate for purchases effective prior to 10/10/22	Higher Residential Tax Rate* (since 01/12/20)
Up to £180,000	0%	0%	4%
The next £45,000 (the portion from £180,001 to £225,000)	0%	3.5%	7.5%
The next £25,000 (the portion from £225,001 to £250,000)	6%	3.5%	7.5%
The next £150,000 (the portion from £250,001 to £400,000)	6%	5%	9%
The next £350,000 (the portion from £400,001 to £750,000)	7.5%	7.5%	11.5%

Purchase price, etc. – Residential Properties	LTT Rate for purchases effective 10/10/22 onwards	LTT Rate for purchases effective prior to 10/10/22	Higher Residential Tax Rate* (since 01/12/20)
The next £750,000 (the portion from £750,001 to £1.5 million)	10%	10%	**14%**
The remaining amount (the portion above £1.5 million)	12%	12%	**16%**

*While the HRAD and ADS for SDLT and LBTT respectively may be considered a surcharge for acquiring a residential property that is not one's main home, etc., elsewhere in the UK, the Welsh Higher Residential Rates were **not** adjusted to align with the Main Residential Rate changes that took effect from 10 October 2022, following the UK's Growth Plan SDLT announcements. They may therefore be considered as *the* rate applicable for company acquisitions, etc.

2. Choosing the Right Structure

Anyone wishing to run a business in the UK has a wide choice of ways to organise it. Each possible structure has its own advantages and disadvantages.

This chapter gives an overview of the three basic types of business structure that are commonly used.

2.1. The Basics: Sole Trader – "One Man Band"

This is the simplest form of business.

A sole trader owns and runs his or her business directly – he or she is "self-employed". All the risks and rewards are his directly, and all the decisions about the business are his.

If things go well he or she owns all the profits that have been made (after having paid tax on them!).

However, if things go badly the sole trader is liable for all the debts of the business. We call this "**un**limited liability" – if the sole trader's business fails, his private property can be taken to pay off the debts of the business. In other words, even his personal wealth outside of his business is at risk.

In summary, there is no real distinction or 'barrier' between the individual and his or her "one man band" business.

2.2. The Basics: Partnership

Where two or more people own and run a business together on a commercial basis, they are generally referred to as operating in partnership.

Like a sole trader, all the risks and rewards belong to the partners – but the crucial point is that, in an ordinary or general partnership, EACH partner is JOINTLY liable for ALL of the partnership's debts.

If things go wrong, any money owed by the partnership business can be recovered from the partners themselves – and if one of them has no money to pay, the other partners will have to pay that person's share of the debts as well. Like the sole trader, a partner's liability is "unlimited" – even non-business personal wealth is at risk.

Note that the Scottish treatment for partnerships differs from the rest of the UK in some aspects of partnership law (although this makes little difference in terms of partnership taxation).

There are also some more specialised forms of partnership that can restrict a partner's potential exposure or liability, which we shall cover in more detail below.

2.3. The Basics: Limited Company

A Limited Company is a "legal person". This means that it exists independently of its owners – its shareholders – and it can make contracts, and be sued for its debts in its own name and on its own behalf.

Here, the word "Limited" means that the shareholders' liability is <u>limited</u> to the money they have invested in their shares. If things go wrong then, in the vast majority of cases, the worst that can happen to the shareholders is that they will not get their share money back - though as we shall see, this is not *always* the case (see 12.9 below). **Notwithstanding those exceptions, limited liability is one of the key non-tax reasons why someone might choose to run their business through a company.**

One of the key consequences of this legal distinction is that a company's money does not automatically 'belong' to its owners (shareholders) in the way that it does with one man bands and ordinary partnerships, as noted above. Even if you own all of the shares in your own company, its assets – including its cash – are primarily the legal property of the company. How the company decides to transfer its wealth to its owners, etc., is what we shall look at in more detail, in the coming chapters.

2.4. Types of Partnerships – or is it a Joint Venture?

Having gone through the basics, we shall now drill down into partnerships, for a bit more detail. There is really only one kind of sole trader, but there are different kinds of partnership.

The basic type of partnership is defined by the Partnership Act 1890, and involves "persons carrying on a business in common with a view of profit".

A partnership is not a separate legal person from its members, and for tax purposes it is "transparent". In other words, the partnership itself does not pay tax – each partner pays tax on his or her share of the profits.

(In Scotland, a partnership *is* a legal person, but for tax purposes, it is treated in the same way as an English partnership, and is "transparent" like them).

In some cases, although two people may agree to share the income from a project, they are not strictly a partnership because they are not carrying on "a business in common".

In such a case, the activity is commonly referred to as a "joint venture".

HM Revenue and Customs (HMRC) will sometimes claim that this is the case where one or more jointly owned properties are rented out, and this distinction can have significant tax consequences, as we shall see later in 12.1. (For further information on whether a co-owned property letting business is operating merely as a joint investment activity or as a 'proper' partnership, please see our separate report, "Taxation of Property Partnerships and Joint Ownership").

We have noted above that the partners in a partnership are jointly liable for the business debts.

There are, however, some varieties of partnership where this does not apply, and these are detailed in the following sections.

2.4.1. A "Limited Partnership"

A "Limited Partnership" is a type of partnership where one or more of the partners has his or her liability limited to the capital he contributes to the partnership when he joins – like a shareholder, the worst that can happen to him is that he loses the money he invested, unlike an ordinary partner who might lose everything.

There are special rules for such partnerships:

- At least one of the partners must be a "general partner" who has **un**limited liability, as with an ordinary partnership, and is responsible for running the business.

- A limited partner is not allowed to withdraw any of his or her capital from the partnership until he leaves the firm.

- A limited partner is not allowed to take part in running the partnership's business, or to make contracts, etc., on behalf of the firm – if he does, he loses his limited liability and becomes an ordinary or general partner.

- There are restrictions on how much tax relief such partners can have for any losses made by the partnership, and they cannot get tax relief for the interest on any money they borrow to invest in the partnership.

Such partnerships are rather specialised entities, but they can have their uses.

Case Study - 1   A "Limited Partnership"

Mary wants to set up a new business, and her Aunt Sally is prepared to invest 60% of the capital needed to help her, in exchange for a fair share of the profits.

She doesn't want to have "unlimited liability" so the obvious solution seems to be a company, but Mary would rather not incur the expense of setting up and running one.

Instead, the new business is set up as a limited partnership, with Mary as the General Partner and Sally as the Limited Partner.

This way, Sally has limited liability, as she would have had with a company.

In other words, a limited partner must be a "sleeping partner" – that is, a partner who does not get involved in running the partnership.

2.4.2. A Limited Liability Partnership (also referred to as an "LLP")

This is a relatively new sort of business entity, which was made possible by the Limited Liability Partnership Act 2000.

Unlike a normal partnership, it is a separate legal person from its members, but for tax purposes it is basically "transparent" like an ordinary partnership – each partner pays tax personally on his or her share of the partnership's profits.

As the name implies, the partners in an LLP have limited liability, like shareholders in a company.

LLPs have proved popular with large professional firms such as accountants and solicitors, but as a general rule they may not be appropriate for the smallest property investors or traders, being rather cumbersome to administer.

The idea of LLPs was that they would combine the advantages of a company (perhaps most importantly, limited liability) with those of a partnership (informality and flexibility).

Some would say, however, that they also combine the disadvantages!

Except for unusual situations (like Case Study - 1, where one party wanted to invest but not to be actively involved), the most suitable form of partnership for the property investor is likely to be the traditional or general Partnership Act type, as described above. But a Limited Liability Partnership may offer a useful alternative in some cases, for example a potentially "risky" property development project, where the partners or "members" might want to limit their personal liability exposure. In many cases, however, the limited company may offer a straightforward alternative.

3. Getting to Grips with Limited Companies

In this chapter we will start to understand the structure of Limited Companies.

3.1. The Different Types of Limited Company

There are several types of Limited Company:

A Private Limited Company is the type we shall be concentrating on in this guide. It is the basic type of limited company, used by hundreds of thousands of businesses.

A Public Limited Company ("plc.") is allowed to raise funds by selling shares to the public, but it is also subject to much stricter legal controls than a Private Limited Company.

A Listed Company is a plc. whose shares can be traded on the Stock Exchange.

There are some other types of company, such as a **company limited by guarantee** – this is normally used by charities, and because it is not allowed to distribute its profits to its shareholders, it is ideal for that purpose – and useless for a property investor!

> For the rest of this guide, when we use the word "company" we shall be referring to a **private limited company**.

3.2. The Basic Rules for a Company

The basic rules for a company are:

- It must have at least one shareholder. The shareholders own the company, and their ownership is evidenced by the number of **shares** they own. If, for example, a company has a total of 100 shares issued to its shareholders, someone who owns 51 of those shares owns 51% of the company.

    He or she also **"controls"** the company, because in normal circumstances he will have 51 out of 100 votes if decisions are to be made about the company's policies.

    Hence in general terms, a 51% "controlling interest" is worth much more than a 49% "minority interest", even though only 2% voting power separates them.

- It must have at least one director. Directors are responsible for running the company's business affairs. The shareholders own the company, but the directors run it on a day to day basis. In the case of the typical smaller property business company, the directors are often the shareholders as well.

- A company must prepare and file accounts each year with Companies House (the government agency that regulates UK companies). These must be filed within 9 months of the end of the period covered by the accounts.

- A company must also file various returns of other information with Companies House, notifying such things as the appointment of new directors, and so on.

- A Company must have a **Memorandum and Articles of Association.** These are formal documents which set out the basic structure of the company – the number of shares it can issue, the rules for transferring shares from one person to another, and the purposes for which the company has been formed.

    Although these "Memo & Articles" are available as standard format documents, it is important to be sure that they are appropriate for your particular company.

    If necessary, the "Memo & Articles" can be altered or updated, but there is a formal process for doing this.

- Decisions made by the directors or shareholders of a company should be recorded in the company's **Minutes** – which comprise a formal record of such things as appointing new directors, issuing shares, or paying dividends.

    There is an example of a company **minute** in section 7.4.1 of this guide.

If this sounds a daunting list of tasks, do not despair – there are a number of specialist companies that offer help with the more unusual tasks, and your accountant will be able to advise you on compliance with the routine requirements.

> It is important to bear in mind, however, that a company is a more formal structure than a sole trader or a partnership, and that there are penalties for failing to comply with the rules.

The accounts of a company must be prepared according to certain rules and in a certain format. **You will need an accountant to prepare these for you.**

Companies whose size exceeds two out of the three following thresholds are also required to have their accounts "audited" – that is, checked for accuracy by an independent accountant. These thresholds were increased in 2016 to:

- a turnover of over £10.2 million,
- assets of more than £5.1 million,
- an average of over 50 employees

Even if your company falls below these limits and an audit is not required, you should include the cost of having company accounts prepared by an accountant when you look at the figures for your company.

All the above requirements for companies mean that you should budget for additional "compliance" costs for each year – to cover preparation of formal accounts, submission of the various statutory returns, and working out the tax payable by the company; also the time taken up by dealing with the additional paperwork.

Previously, we have suggested that a flat £1,000pa might suffice but in this edition, we have dropped the presumption of a fixed cost, as it is likely to be quite variable for different businesses – see also Appendix B.

Once a company has filed its accounts, they become **public information.**

Anyone (including your employees or your competitors) can access Companies House' website and get a copy of previously-filed accounts, together with information on the shareholders and directors of the company.

For companies that are excused from being audited, only "abridged" or "filleted" accounts (previously referred to as "abbreviated" accounts) need be filed and made public – "abridged" accounts do not show as much detail as full accounts (for example there may not be a profit and loss account) but even so, they give quite a lot of information about the company.

So far, these additional constraints are fairly well-established. But the Economic Crime and Corporate Transparency Act 2023 introduced a range of new rules for 2024, including:

- Companies can no longer a PO Box address for their registered office
- Companies will also have to register an e-mail address so that Companies House may communicate with them
- A new company must include a formal declaration that it is being formed for a legal purpose, while all companies will have to confirm that their future activities will be lawful in their annual Confirmation Statements
- Enhanced data sharing between other government departments and with law enforcement agencies

Further measures, such as requiring enhanced ID verification measures for company officers, are intended to follow. This should help to prevent companies from being "hijacked" – where a third party, purporting to be an authorised officer of the company, changes details to wrest control of it from the legitimate owners / officers. More widely, it should also help to prevent less-savoury characters from using companies to carry out frauds or similar crimes. The extent of the additional burden on ordinary law-abiding companies / officers remains to be seen.

4. Understanding Corporation Tax

In this chapter we will understand the meaning of Corporation Tax ("CT") and will look at how this tax affects companies.

4.1. The Rates of Corporation Tax

With effect from 1 April 2015, practically all companies paid UK Corporation Tax ("CT") on their profits – including their capital gains – at the same rate. This fell from 20% to 19% for profits arising after March 2017. The government recently scrapped its long-term plans to reduce the CT rate to 17% from April 2020, and then announced that it would be raised back up to 25% from April 2023, essentially as follows:

Profits Band	Rate up to 31 March 2023	*Effective* Rate from 1 April 2023
£0 - £50,000	19.0%	19.0%
£50,001 - £250,000	19.0%	26.5%
£250,001+	19.0%	25.0%

The change in rates will in some cases significantly affect the net benefit of incorporation, when compared to running the same business as a one-man band, or partnership.

As a simple example, a company with £200,000 of taxable profits would enjoy only 19% CT on the first £50,000 of those profits, but then suffer a quite punitive 26.5% rate on the remaining £150,000. This would equate to an effective overall rate of 24.6%. The particularly high "marginal rate" in the middle is intended to increasingly offset the generous initial 19% rate as profits rise, so that by the time a company's taxable profits reach £250,000, it is as if the company has been paying 25% all along.

See the tables in Appendix B for further consideration of how changing rates affect incorporation at various profit levels, etc.

Note also that, given that companies pay the same rate of Corporation Tax on capital gains as on ordinary profits, then the recently-announced reduction in the higher rate of CGT applicable to individuals, to (non-corporate) partners in a partnership and to Trusts, from 28% down to 24% for disposals effective on or after 6 April 2024, means that companies will likely pay slightly more any substantial capital gains than do individuals, etc. (see 5.1 for an example).

4.2. Associated Companies – Anti-Fragmenting Regime

For the last several years, there was only one main rate of Corporation Tax – 19% - so there was no need for the "associated companies" regime. Now that we have profits bands again, the associated companies rules are back, and for older advisers, it's almost like they've never been away. The "associated companies" rules are meant to dissuade business owners from fragmenting or splitting their business into several companies, by apportioning the company tax bands across companies under common control.

Given that taxable profits above £50,000 are taxed more highly than those below the threshold, business owners might be tempted to set up several smaller companies to replace their single business. For example, a landlady with 20 similar properties making £200,000pa in rental profits might set up 5 limited companies, that she owns outright, each company with 4 properties and making £40,000 profits annually.

Setting to one side the complexities and process of incorporating the business in the first place, this is acceptable in terms of general law, but when it comes to **taxing** the companies, they will each have only 1/5th of the Small Profits Band of £50,000 allocated to them, so each of the 5 companies will enjoy the 19% rate for only the first £10,000 of their total profits of around £40,000. The companies are deemed to be "associated" – that is, they are all under "common control" of the same person, or person**s** (so it will not make things any better, tax-wise, if the companies' ownership is spread out amongst close family). "Control" can be identified by various means, but most commonly by securing the greater part of:
- Share capital
- Voting Rights
- Rights to income, or to the company's assets on a winding-up

The rules for associated companies used to be widely drawn, and catch spouses or civil partners each running their own entirely separate limited companies. Fortunately, the latest version of the regime will only combine the rights and powers of associates to derive common control where there is "**substantial commercial interdependence**" between the companies being considered. The companies can be:

Financially interdependent – such as where one company gives financial support to the other, or
Economically interdependent – overlapping businesses such as where one company's activities will benefit the other, or they share customers
Organisationally interdependent– the companies share premises, employees, equipment, etc.

Associate Companies – Tax "Penalty"

Where companies *are* associated, the Corporation Tax outcome can in some scenarios be worse than if they were a single company running the businesses together.

Companies can be associated but not be in a group. If one company makes a tax loss, it cannot simply be set against an associated company's profits (unless they also happen both to be in the same **group** for tax purposes – "Group Relief")
If one company makes a lot of profit but another associate makes small profits, then some of the total Small Profits Band will likely be wasted.

Example

Elsa has a property development trading company that makes £60,000 profit annually. In the year to 31 December 2024, the company's Corporation Tax will be:

	£		£	£
Profits at Small Companies Rate	50,000	@ 19.0% =	9,500	
Profits at Marginal Rate	10,000	@ 26.5%	2,650	
	60,000			12,150

Olaf owns two property development companies outright – they are therefore under common control and are associated companies (they are both under the control of the same "person", so it does not matter whether or not there is "substantial commercial interdependence" between the companies, although it might if Olaf owned one and his civil partner Rudolph owned the other). Company S1 makes only £15,000 annually, while Company S2 makes £45,000 annually. In the year to 31 December 2025, the companies' Corporation Tax will be:

	£			£	£
Company S1					
Profits at Small Companies Rate	15,000	@	19.0% =	2,850	
Profits at Marginal Rate	-	@	26.5%	-	
	15,000				2,850
Company S2					
Profits at Small Companies Rate	25,000	@	19.0% =	4,750	
Profits at Marginal Rate	20,000	@	26.5%	5,300	
	45,000				10,050
					12,900

Despite Olaf's companies enjoying the same taxable profits in aggregate as Elsa's single company, his have the higher Corporation Tax bill overall, because Company S1 is not making enough taxable profit to fully utilise the £25,000 Small Profits Band available to it, and more profit is taxed in Company S2 at the higher Marginal Rate of 26.5%.

4.3. Key Dates for the Company

A company must decide on the date to which it will prepare its accounts – its **accounting reference date.**

A company normally has the same accounting reference date every year, so that its **period of account** is the year ending on that accounting reference date.

If a company wishes, it can change its accounting reference date, so that the period covered by its formal financial statements is longer or shorter than one year – but it cannot be longer than 18 months (this is set by Company law, rather than tax law).

For the purposes of corporation tax, companies are taxed on the profits they make in their **accounting period.**

This is normally the same as the company's period of account, so that if a company's accounting date is 31 December (the most popular date, along with 31 March) then its period of account will be the year ending on 31 December, and its accounting period for Corporation Tax purposes will also be the year ending 31 December.

In some circumstances, there may be a difference between the company's period of account and its accounting period. This is because the tax legislation includes rules for when a company's taxable accounting period ends, and these mean that an accounting period for tax purposes may end on a different day to the company's accounting date.

For Corporation Tax purposes, a company's accounting period comes to an end at the **earliest** of several dates, including:

- 12 months after it started (whereas a company's accounts may cover up to 18 months, as noted above).

- The date the company chooses as its accounting date (so for example, if the accounting period begins on 1 January, and the company decides to change its accounting date to 31 October, it will have a 10-month accounting period for that year).

- The date the company becomes liable to Corporation Tax (such as when it first gets a taxable source of income) – or when it stops being so liable.

- The date the company begins trading.

- The date the company stops trading.

- The date the **winding up** of the company begins (that is, when the process of ending the company's existence starts).

In cases where the company's accounting period (for tax) is not the same as its period of account, the tax inspector will expect profits to be apportioned across the period of account to arrive at the profits of the accounting period – this most often happens when the company's period of account is longer than one year.

The apportionment is normally done on a time basis, but the inspector (or the company) can look at the dates of specific transactions if this gives a fairer result – for example, if a large part of a car-dealing company's profit for a long period of account came from one transaction, such as the sale of a vintage Ferrari, this could be put wholly into the tax accounting period when it occurred rather than being apportioned or "spread" across more than one period.

4.4. Benefiting from the Favourable Company Taxes

Rates of tax for companies may seem very favourable, compared to Income Tax at 40% for taxable income over roughly £50,270, (including the tax-free Personal Allowance), and as much as 45% for taxable income over £125,140.

Case Study - 2   Favourable Company Taxes

Bill has a property portfolio of 10 buy to let properties, within his own company – he is director and 100% shareholder.

After all expenses, the rentals from these properties produce a profit of £20,000 per year. Because the portfolio is held within a company, the company must pay CT of £3,800 (£20,000 at 19%). Bill owns and controls no other companies.

If Bill owned the properties directly, the Income Tax he would pay would depend on how much other income he had for the year, but it would probably be between £4,000 (£20,000 at 20%) and £8,000 (£20,000 at 40%).

> Note that, because profits are below £50,000 for the year, this does **not** change after April 2023 (see 4.1)

> The above simple case study, however, misses out one of the most important tax aspects of companies, as compared to sole traders or partnerships: once the company has paid its CT for the year, the remaining cash still belongs to the company, not (yet) its shareholders/directors, and there may be further tax costs in extracting it – sometimes referred to as "the double tax charge".

4.5. Extracting the Cash from the Company

There are essentially two ways of extracting cash from a company, on an ongoing basis, and both these methods are described in the following sections. (We look at extracting the accumulated capital from a business at the end of its life – or when you want to retire from it – in Chapter 16; see also 12.8 for an example of a company that has been set up for a specific project).

4.5.1. *Paying a Salary*

If a company wants to pay either a regular salary or make ad hoc wages payments to its director(s), it will have to set up a PAYE scheme just like any other employer, and account for the PAYE and National Insurance Contributions (NICs) – including Employers' NICs – on such payments just as it would with ordinary employees. Under "Real Time Information" ("RTI") reporting, all payroll transactions must be notified online to HMRC, basically immediately that they are paid, although some of the repetition can be avoided by simply paying the annual salary, in full, once in the year. While it is theoretically possible in some circumstances to avoid setting up a PAYE scheme under RTI, it will be necessary in the majority of cases – especially where the director already has another PAYE source of income, and/or the company wants to pay a 'decent' salary.

There are special rules that apply to directors' salaries, which ensure that NICs are worked out on an annualised basis (in the past, a director could deliberately arrange to pay all of his or her annual salary in one go, which meant effectively paying only a month's worth of NICs; the rules were therefore changed, and now directors generally work on a "tax year to date" basis, and are less able to benefit – NIC-wise – from fluctuating salaries than are ordinary employees).

Case Study - 3   Extracting Money Using a Salary

If Bill has no other income for the year, and the company pays all of its £20,000 profits out to him as a salary, the tax works like this:

Company Profit (after deducting salary)	NIL
Employers' NIC on salary	(1,322)
Salary net of Employers' NIC	18,678
Employees' NIC	(489)
Income tax	(1,222)
Cash in hand after PAYE	16,967
Effective rate of tax on £20,000	15.17%

If Bill had owned the properties directly, then his tax bill would have been:

Income from property	20,000
Deduct Personal Allowance	(12,570)
Taxable income	7,430
Income Tax at 20%	(1,486)
Cash in hand after tax	18,514
Effective rate of tax on £20,000	7.43%

Notes:

1. Employers' NICs are calculated as the employer's separate and additional liability to HMRC for having paid wages.

   If, as an employer, I want to pay someone an annual salary of £20,000, then the gross salary is £20,000, **and** I have to pay Employers' NICs on top, of £1,504; the total cost to me as employer is a gross wage of £20,000 **and** Employers' NICs of £1,504. This comes to £21,504 – i.e., more than £20,000. (The employee's own NICs and Income Tax are taken out of the £20,000, so are not a cost to me as the employer, except that I have to withhold it and pay it over to HMRC).

> In the above example, Bill's company has only £20,000 to cover both the gross salary *and* Employers' NICs, which is why we have to start by deducting the Employers' NICs, to derive how much the company can actually afford to pay Bill as gross salary.
>
> 2. There are minimum thresholds at which an employee's salary becomes subject to Employees' NICs and to Employers' NICs (and any part of Bill's salary paid below those levels escapes the corresponding charge):
>
>   a. Employee's NIC Primary NICs Threshold: £12,570 (£12,570 in 2023/24)
>   b. Employers' NIC Secondary NICs Threshold £9,100 (£9,100 in 2023/24)
>
> 3. There is no National Insurance to pay where the property business is owned personally (rather than through a company), because letting property is not a trade – it does not comprise earnings for NI purposes.
>
>   National insurance *is* payable on the salary from the company, however, as it is on all salaries. In this simple example, we have not considered any extra costs of running the business as a company, and all of the company's rental profits have been paid out as salary + Employers' NICs, so there is no Corporation Tax to pay: taxable profits are £nil.

Directors are also caught by special rules governing *when* a salary is deemed to be paid for PAYE purposes, which in turn determines when PAYE and NICs have to be accounted for. For ordinary employees, the basic rule is that PAYE and NICs are triggered when salary is paid to them, or they become entitled to it (whichever is the earlier). But for directors, salary is deemed to be paid on whichever is the **earliest** of:

- When they become entitled to be paid.
- When they are physically paid (i.e., so far just like ordinary employees) *and*
- The date earnings are credited in the books of the company in relation to a specific director (e.g., it is put through the company's accounting system, for example when it is credited to the director's loan account with the company).
- Where the amount of earnings is determined before the end of the period to which they related, (such as an interim performance bonus), the date that period ends.
- Where the amount of earnings is determined after the end of the period to which they related (such as a bonus which can be determined only once the company's annual profits are known), then the date on which the amount is determined.

The application of these rules can be obvious in some cases but less so in others. **The key point is that if, as a director, you want to defer (postpone) a bonus, etc., for fear of triggering PAYE and NICs too early, make sure to take advice first!**

4.5.2. Paying Dividends Instead

The other way for Bill to extract the cash from his company is for the company to pay him a **dividend**.

A dividend is how a company distributes its profits to its shareholders.

Simply put:

- A dividend is a return on a shareholder's investment, having bought shares in a company

- A salary is a director's reward or remuneration for acting as an officer (simply, an employee) of the company

Bill has the choice of either route because he is both shareholder and director of his own company.

Note that, unlike paying a salary to a director or other employee, a company cannot deduct the dividends it pays from its profits chargeable to CT.

It can be said that paying a salary reduces a company's Corporation Tax liability because it typically reduces the company's taxable profits. But a dividend is paid out of the profits remaining to a company *after* it has settled or otherwise recognised all other financial commitments, including Corporation Tax: dividends are paid out of "post-tax profits".

When individual shareholders receive a dividend, the rate of tax they pay at a personal level depends on their other income for the tax year. The rules for the taxation of dividends changed markedly from April 2016. We use these 'new' rules in this book. If those shareholders are not liable to tax at the higher rate (taxable income exceeding the tax-free Personal Allowance of £12,570 by over £37,700 for 2024/25 – i.e., an aggregate 'floor' of £50,270), then the rate of Income Tax on their dividend is 8.75%

This low rate might seem very generous in isolation, but remember that, since dividends are paid out of *post-tax* profits, the company will already have suffered Corporation Tax before the profits are paid out as dividends taxed on the shareholder.

In the tax years running up to 2015/16, the *effective* tax rate for dividends up to the higher rate threshold was nil; now there is a tax-free Dividend Allowance that covers up to the first £500 of dividend income (it was initially set at £5,000 but subsequent Chancellors have decided that was *far* too generous), so to summarise:

Rate	2024/25*	2021/22	2015/16
"Allowance" (first £500)	0%	0%	N/A
Ordinary Rate above £12,570 next £37,700	8.75%	7.50%	0.00%
Higher Rate between £50,270 and £125,140	33.75%	32.50%	25.00%
Additional Rate above £125,140	39.35%	38.10%	30.56%

*Includes the extra 1.25% additional Dividend Income Tax from 6 April 2022.

Where someone is already a Basic Rate taxpayer, typically because they have already used their tax-free Personal Allowance against other taxable income, but there is enough left of the next band to cover their dividend income, then the calculation will be as follows:

Basic Rate Taxpayer already	
Dividend paid	10,000
Less: Dividend Allowance	(500)
Taxable amount of dividend	9,500
Income tax on dividend at 8.75%	831

Note: Prior to 2016/17, there would have been **no** tax to pay on a dividend received by a basic rate taxpayer.

If the shareholder is already liable to Income Tax at the Higher Rate, then the rate of tax on their £10,000 dividend will be the "Dividend Upper Income rate" of 33.75%, and they still get the Dividend Allowance, so it works like this:

Higher Rate Taxpayer already	
Dividend paid	10,000
Less: Dividend Allowance	(500)
Taxable amount of dividend	9,500
Income tax on dividend at 33.75%	3,206

Note: Prior to 2016/17, the old rules would have meant that a Higher Rate taxpayer would have paid only £2,500 on a taxable cash dividend of £10,000. (There was also no Dividend Allowance before 2016/17).

Case Study - 4   Extracting Money Using a Dividend Instead of Salary

Mrs Mean hates paying tax. For years, she has taken dividends up to the higher rate threshold and paid no tax. Based on the old dividend rules, she could have taken around £38,000 in dividends in 2015/16 and paid no tax.

She arranges for her company to pay her a dividend in 2024/25 of £50,270, (Including the standard tax-free Personal Allowance of £12,570 for 2024/25, the Higher Rate Threshold for this tax year is £50,270) Unfortunately for Mrs. Mean, the new dividend rules apply:

Mrs Mean	
Dividend paid	50,270
Deduct Dividend Allowance	(500)
Deduct standard Personal Allowance	(12,570)
Taxable dividend income	37,200
Dividend taxable at 8.75%	3,255

Mrs. Mean will no doubt be upset that she is liable for £3,255 tax on her £50,270 dividend in 2024/25. However, if the company were to pay her a gross salary of £50,270 out of its profits instead, the combination of Income Tax and National Insurance would cost around £4,600 extra, even after factoring in the savings in Corporation Tax of paying a salary instead of dividends – because of Employees' NIC and Employers' NIC, as well as tax.

It seems clear, then, that dividends rather than salary are often the way to extract cash from a company – but there can be cases where a mixture of the two provides the best solution.

4.5.3.   Paying Dividends and a Salary

Case Study - 5   Extracting Money Using Both Dividend and a Salary (1)

Bill's property company makes a profit of £20,000 per year (see case study 3).

Bill has no other income for the year, so he pays himself a salary which is just below the "threshold" for Income Tax and Employees' NIC*. The rest of the profit is paid out as a dividend:

	Company	Cash for Bill
Profit	20,000	
Deduct salary*	(12,570)	12,570
Deduct Employers' NICs	(479)	
Profit after salary	6,951	
Deduct CT on profit (19%)	(1,321)	
Profit after tax (dividend)	5,630	
Tax on Dividend	(449)	5,181
Total cash for Bill		17,752
Effective rate of tax	11.24%	

Bill has lost around £760 more tax compared to the position if he had owned these properties directly (see the second part of Case Study 3) and, in reality, he would also have had to pay the additional costs of running a company.

*The lowest threshold at which Income Tax or NICs become payable in 2024/25 is £9,100, as it is the lowest of:

Threshold	2024/25	(2023/24)
Personal Allowance	12,570	(12,570)
Employee's NIC (annualised for directors, etc.)	12,570	(12,570)
Employers' NIC	9,100	(9,100)

Employ*er* NICs will be payable as soon as earnings exceed £9,100 in the year. However, as the only cost between £9,100 and £12,570 is Employ*ers'* NICs, typically it is slightly cheaper overall to take salary up to £12,570, which is the maximum before Employ*ees'* NICs also become payable.

In broad terms, a company is unlikely to save enough money for a basic rate taxpayer for incorporation to be worthwhile (unless he has significant borrowings and therefore mortgage interest to pay on residential properties – see Chapter 6).

Now let us look at the position for a higher rate taxpayer:

Case Study - 6   Extracting Money Using Both Dividend and a Salary (2)

Ben has other (non-dividend) income which means he pays Income Tax at the 40% Higher Rate (or 33.75% for dividends). He also has a property portfolio in a company which, like Bill's, yields £20,000 profit per year.

He uses the same strategy as Bill in Case Study 5, paying himself a salary just below the "threshold":

	Company	Cash for Ben
Profit	20,000	
Deduct salary	(12,570)	12,570
Deduct Employers' NICs	(479)	
Profit after salary	6,951	
Deduct CT on profit (19%)	(1,321)	
Profit after tax (dividend)	5,630	
Income tax on dividend	(1,731)	3,899
Total cash for Ben		16,469
Effective rate of tax	17.66%	

If Ben had owned the properties directly, he would have paid 40% tax on the £20,000 profit (£8,000) and made £12,000, so he has apparently saved £4,469.

Because he has used £12,570 of his tax-free personal allowance against *this salary*, however, he will pay £5,028 more tax on his other (non-property) income, so he is actually slightly (£560!) worse off – but this is *before* factoring in the nominal extra £1,000 cost of running the company. (We are also ignoring any potential impact on the Savings Allowance" for bank and building society interest, which would further complicate matters).

> (Strictly, the effective marginal tax rates are such that Bill would actually be slightly better off if he took only £9,100 salary – limiting himself to the point at which Employers' NIC became payable – but the difference would be less than £40 and he would still be worse off overall. We have kept the salary at £12,570, for ease of comparison.)

The position would be worse if Ben decided to pay himself all in dividends. If so, the calculation would be:

	Company	Cash for Ben
Profit	20,000	
Deduct CT on profit	(3,800)	
Profit after tax (dividend)	16,200	
Income tax on dividend	(5,299)	
Total cash for Ben		10,901
Effective rate of tax	45.50%	

Although we are no longer "borrowing" £5,028 of salary tax against Personal Allowance used elsewhere, (because Ben is not taking a salary in this example), his net income of £10,901 is still £1,099 worse than if he'd just owned the rental portfolio directly and paid 40% Income Tax on all rental profits – and that is, again, before we consider the additional cost of running a company. However, taking a combination of salary and dividends still yields a better outcome than taking the profits through dividends alone.

4.5.4. Are Dividends Always Better?

While a sole or "singleton" director/shareholder will typically always benefit from having a modest salary topped up with dividends, there may be more complex scenarios where taking a further salary instead of dividends could actually be marginally be more tax-efficient. This is a new development and may apply only in quite unusual circumstances.

The calculations are long-winded, and quite finely balanced with only small marginal savings, but the higher rates of Corporation Tax can now be so punitive that paying a bonus in salary – that reduces the company's tax bill because it is "tax-deductible" – can effectively save more Corporation Tax than the director/shareholder would save in personal tax, if they were taking a dividend instead. The combinations to look out for are where:

- The director is already a higher-rate taxpayer **before** counting their dividend income (say because they have significant income from other sources), and

- The company is profits are sufficiently high that it is paying Corporation Tax at the higher rates – the Marginal Rate of 26.5%, or the Main Rate of 25.0%

Best advice is to check with your adviser, when contemplating a significant bonus or similar payment, to ensure that the timing and composition of salary and/or dividend is optimised. There may even be alternatives, such as benefits or pension contributions, that can work better in some cases.

4.6. Beyond the Basics

We have looked at the annual tax on profits position for companies and found that the outcomes when compared to the original unincorporated or "self-employed" models has become quite finely balanced. In certain situations, however, it can still produce savings, as we shall soon see in the coming chapters. Please see also the Tables in Appendix B, which lists anticipated savings or costs for incorporating a property investment business, at various profit/net income levels.

Notwithstanding that Corporation Tax rates are still relatively low when compared to the Income Tax / NICs that would be payable on equivalent profits by unincorporated businesses, the individual will also have to pay Income Tax and potentially NICs on any salary taken, or Income Tax alone on dividends. We call this a "double tax charge"

However, the standard model makes some important assumptions:

- The individual director/shareholder has no other significant sources of income

- The individual director/shareholder needs to extract all of the profits generated – no matter how high – to support their ongoing private income needs on an indefinite basis

- The properties are all normal residential "Buy-to-Lets"

- Longer-term tax issues, such as Inheritance Tax, are not involved

These assumptions are important because they promote a consistent approach and make it possible to compare one year with another, and one business with another, etc. But in reality, few businesses will stand still for long enough that profits made in 2015/16 will correlate neatly with those made in 2024/25: the portfolio may well grow or contract; the landlord's own priorities may well also change over time.

To summarise some key advantages for now:

Income Retention - Where the individual does **not** need to withdraw all of the company's post-Corporation Tax profits to fund their personal income needs, they will pay less Income Tax – there will be less exposure to the double tax charge. It also means that there will be more profits left in the business to fund:

- Further growth (see 5.1) or

- Capital extraction typically at the end of the company's life and subject to Capital Gains Tax at a rate as low as 10% (see Chapter 16)

- A cash box company to operate as a rudimentary pension – see Chapter 16 and in particular Case Study - 36– Living Off the Profits

Pensions – Where the individual is a property investor/landlord and wants to make significant pension contributions, then the company can make such payments on their behalf in a tax-efficient manner – see 14.5

Useful Benefits - There are also several other benefits that a company can provide tax-efficiently as the employer (see again 14.5)

Capital Allowances – these access tax relief for investing in qualifying "fixed assets" such as plant, machinery, office equipment and electrical systems. The average BTL property investor will have little scope to claim extensive Capital Allowances because they are prohibited in dwellings that are let out to tenants (so a typical landlord might claim for their home office, power tools or similar).

But it is not uncommon to find that 12%+ of the purchase price of a modern **commercial** building is eligible for Capital Allowances, after taking into consideration such candidates as:

- Electrical wiring
- Lighting
- Telecommunications and IT infrastructure
- Heating
- Air-conditioning
- Kitchens and washrooms, including white goods and sanitaryware
- Office furniture

The new "full-expensing" of Capital Allowances (see 1.1) that typically allows 100% tax relief is available **only to companies**, with no upper limit, making companies potentially much more tax-efficient than unincorporated entities, for serious investors in commercial property (i.e., for investments beyond the £1million pa Annual Investment Allowance that is more widely available).

5. Building Up a Property Portfolio Using a Company

In this chapter, we will look at when it is beneficial to use a company to **grow** a property portfolio, tax-efficiently.

5.1. Using a Company to Grow Your Property Portfolio

A company comes into its own when the plan is to keep the profits in the company, such as for reinvesting into more property, rather than to draw them out for living expenses.

Jane has a well-paid job, and pays Income Tax at 40%.

She wants to build up a portfolio of residential properties, using the profits from the rentals to fund the acquisition of other properties.

She begins with a portfolio of 10 buy to let properties in 2025, like Bill's, but instead of taking the profits out of the company, she leaves them there to fund the deposits on new properties.

In the first year, the position will be:

	Company	Direct ownership
Profits	20,000	20,000
Tax payable	(3,800)	(8,000)
Cash for reinvestment	16,200	12,000

If the pattern is repeated in the following years, it is clear that she will be able to spend more money (within the company) on investing in new properties than she would if she were paying Income Tax on the rents. This relative saving will result in a "virtuous cycle", whereby each year can result in better and better results, thanks to the lower Corporate Tax rate.

In (say) 2030, Jane's company sells some of its properties. The disposals are subject to Corporation Tax on capital gains:

	Company	Direct ownership
Proceeds	400,000	400,000
Cost of properties	(200,000)	(200,000)
Capital Gain	200,000	200,000

Tax payable (26.5% / 24%*)	(53,000)	(48,000)
Cash for reinvestment	347,000	352,000

*Note that, with the reduction in the higher rate of CGT from 28% down to 24% that took effect for personal disposals from 6 April 2024, Jane's company will pay slightly more tax on the capital gain than she would personally. (We are assuming in the CGT calculation that Jane has already used her personal Annual Exemption).

Note also that Jane would normally have to pay more tax to personally access those funds in the company – the so-called "double tax charge" – where the company pays tax on profits or gains, and then the shareholder/director pays tax to get the funds out of the company for personal use.

But these calculations serve to illustrate how companies will usually have the ongoing advantage if they are able to retain their profits, year on year, to boost growth. This will normally apply only if a landlord or landlady has sufficient other income or wealth – or a portfolio of sufficient size – that he or she can afford to the leave most profits (if not all) in the company wrapper.

However, there is a recent development that will, for many **residential** landlords, tip the balance strongly in favour of incorporation, whether they keep the profits in the company or not. That is the disallowance of finance costs in relation to the letting of residential property, which we shall look at next.

6. Disallowance of Mortgage Interest on Residential Properties

This measure was announced in the 2015 Summer Budget, and has been outraging residential property landlords ever since.

Generally, costs are fully deductible so long as they relate to the business – they are incurred "wholly and exclusively" for the property business (or are apportioned if appropriate, such as where only some of the expense is applied for business purposes). But since April 2017, (the 2017/18 tax year), interest relief has gradually been disallowed for tax purposes only.

The key points are:
- The regime applies to all taxpayers that pay **Income Tax** – individuals, partners, and trusts but **not** companies (which currently pay as little as 19% Corporation Tax anyway – but see 4.1).
- It applies to any kind of financing deal, not just a simple 'mortgage'.
- It applies to any kind of finance cost, not just 'interest'.
- It applies to residential properties; commercial properties are ignored.
- Where there are borrowings against both commercial and residential properties, the amount to be disallowed should be apportioned on a "just and reasonable basis".
- While property **developers** are not generally caught, someone financing the development of a property with the intention of ultimately letting it out, rather than for onward sale, **is** potentially caught by the new rules.
- Each tax year from 2017/18 through to 2020/21, a further 25% of the landlord's finance costs has been disallowed, to be replaced by a maximum 20% tax "credit", (strictly, a reduction in his or her tax bill), regardless of the landlord's actual marginal tax rate.

Case Study - 7   Disallowance of Mortgage Interest on Properties

Andrea has a portfolio of almost 20 residential properties that, up 'til now, have been generating around £60,000 of net rental profits – after £80,000 of annual mortgage interest. She is therefore already a 40% taxpayer, despite having no other income. Assuming everything else stays broadly consistent throughout the implementation phase of the new regime (so using 2016/17 rates throughout for ease of comparison to the year just before the new regime starts):

In 2016/17, Andrea will have paid tax on £60,000 – the last year before the new rules started to 'bite'.

In 2017/18, she will have paid tax on profits of £60,000 + (25% x £80,000 in annual interest) = £80,000. The extra £20,000 will have been taxed at 40%, costing £8,000 in tax. She did, however, get a tax credit of 20% x £20,000 = £4,000, so in 2017/18 she owed a further net amount of **£4,000** in tax.

In 2018/19, she will have paid tax on profits of £60,000 + (50% x £80,000 in annual interest) = £100,000. The extra £40,000 will have been taxed at 40%, costing £16,000 in tax. She did get a tax credit of 20% x £40,000 = £8,000, so by 2018/19 she owed a further **£8,000** in tax (compared to 2016/17).

In 2019/20, she will have paid tax on profits of £60,000 + (75% x £80,000) = £120,000. The extra £60,000 will have been taxed at 40%, but she will also have forfeited most of her tax-free Personal Allowance because, for tax purposes only, she has exceeded £100,000 income. This will end up having cost £28,000 in tax. She will still have received a tax credit of 20% x £60,000 = £12,000, so in 2019/20 she owed a further **£16,000** in tax (against 2016/17). **Note the significant increase in tax liability this year, as the tax adjustment cost her most of her Personal Allowance.**

In 2020/21, she will have paid tax on profits of £60,000 + (100% x £80,000) = £140,000. The extra £80,000 would have been taxed at 40%, but she will also have forfeited the last of her tax-free Personal Allowance because, for tax purposes only, she exceeded £100,000 income. This will end up costing £36,400 in tax. She will have received a tax credit of 20% x £80,000 = £16,000, so in 2020/21 she will have owed a further **£20,400** in tax (compared to 2016/17).

So, by the time these new measures have been fully implemented, Andrea's tax bill has risen by £20,400 – roughly 150% – even though her real profits have not moved. Given that companies are not "caught" by this new regime, it will come as no surprise that they offer a relatively safe haven to landlords who might otherwise face the very real prospect of catastrophic business failure.

The above model used 2016/17 rates, etc., throughout to explain the concept. A more accurate summary using later rates and allowances as known, comparing this with the alternative scenario of taking that same business model through a company, with a modest salary of around £8,000 and the balance of available profits as dividends, is set out below:

Tax Year:	2016/17 £	2017/18 £	2018/19 £	2019/20 £	2020/21 £
Net Rent after Mortgage	60,000	60,000	60,000	60,000	60,000
Add-back Rental Finance	0	20,000	40,000	60,000	80,000
Total	60,000	80,000	100,000	120,000	140,000
Net income personally	46,800	43,300	39,640	32,500	27,500
Net if taken through Co.	45,435	46,324	46,462	47,424	47,424
Saving if Co. instead	(1,365)	3,024	6,822	14,924	19,924

Using this model, Andrea's net-of-tax income would have almost halved by 2020/21 if she had continued to run the business on her own account. If she had instead been able to transfer her business into a company, however, it would have been protected from the worst effects of the new regime. For further information, please see Chapter 8 (Offsetting interest charges before 6th April 2017 and Chapter 9 (Offsetting interest charges after 6th April 2017) of the book "How to Avoid Landlord Taxes".

7. Everything You Need to Know About Dividend Payments

We have been talking about companies paying dividends, and it is important to understand the rules that apply to such payments.

In this chapter we will examine these rules more closely.

7.1. Working with "Distributable Profits"

A company can pay a dividend only out of its "distributable profits".

"Distributable profits" are a company's profits **after** paying its expenses, including its corporation tax.

If it does not pay any dividends for a particular year, then those "distributable profits" will remain in the company's balance sheet, and can be used to pay a dividend in later years:

Case Study - 8   Distributing the Profits

A new company is set up, and in its first two years, it makes a profit of £40,000 per year after all expenses. Its distributable profits are therefore:

Profit for year 1	40,000
CT due on profit	(7,600)
Distributable profits	32,400
Profit for year 2	40,000
CT due on profit	(7,600)
Distributable profits	64,800

In the third year, the company has a bad year, and makes a loss of £10,000 after all expenses. Its distributable profits are now:

Distributable profits at start of year	64,800
Deduct loss for year	(10,000)
Repayment of corporation tax on loss	1,900
Distributable profits at end of year	56,700

Things go better in the fourth year, with a profit of £15,000, and the company decides to pay a dividend of £10,000:

Distributable profits at start of year	56,700
Add profit for year	15,000
Deduct CT due on profit	(2,850)
Distributable profits	68,850
Dividend paid	(10,000)
Distributable profits at end of year	58,850

Note that, as the profits in each year are below £50,000, the 19% "Small Companies Rate" applies; higher rates will apply to the extent that the company's taxable profits exceed £50,000pa – see Chapter 4.

7.2. Who Gets the Dividends?

Dividends are paid to the company's shareholders according to how many shares they own – so in a simple case where all the shares are of the same "class", each shareholder gets a dividend proportionate to his or her shareholding.

Case Study - 9   Apportioning the Dividends

The shares in a company are owned as follows:

Mary Jones (wife)	40 £1	Ordinary Shares
Joe Jones (husband)	40 £1	Ordinary Shares
Sue Jones (adult daughter)	20 £1	Ordinary Shares
Total	100 £1	Ordinary Shares

If the company pays a dividend of £10,000, that is equivalent to £100 per share, so the three shareholders will receive:

Mary	£4,000
Joe	£4,000
Sue	£2,000
Total	£10,000

7.3. The Two Types of Dividend

It is important that the formalities are properly observed when a company pays dividends. There are two basic types of dividend:

7.3.1.   *A "Final" Dividend.*

This is a dividend paid out of the company's distributable profits after its accounting period ends.

The shareholders approve the company's accounts for the year, and also approve the payment of a "final" dividend, which is then said to have been "declared".

Although the final dividend may not in fact physically be paid until some time later, it is treated as payable for Income Tax purposes on the day it is "declared" (typically, when the accounts are approved), **unless** the declaration specifies a different date for the actual payment.

7.3.2.   *An "Interim" Dividend.*

This is a dividend paid by a company during the year. It is approved by the directors of the company, who must be satisfied there are enough "distributable reserves" to pay the dividend. For Income Tax purposes, an interim dividend is treated as paid on the date it is actually paid because, broadly speaking, the shareholder cannot enforce payment of an interim dividend (and the directors have the power to revoke payment of an interim dividend right up until it is actually paid).

This was confirmed in the unusual case of Gould v HMRC [2022] UKFTT 00431 (TC), where an interim dividend was paid to the two principal shareholders in different tax years, rather than simultaneously (as would normally be the case).

> It is essential that the directors are satisfied there are sufficient distributable profits before they approve the payment of an interim dividend, and this generally means having accurate and up to date records of the company's income and expenses.
>
> We shall see below what can happen if the directors pay a dividend without taking this precaution.

7.4. Getting the Paperwork Right

It is also essential to produce the correct paperwork for a dividend. This means having:

- A minute of the meeting at which it was decided to pay the dividend.

- A "dividend confirmation" for each shareholder.

7.4.1. Sample – Meeting Minute

Overleaf is a sample wording for the minute of a resolution to pay an interim dividend:

Property Company Limited

Company Registration No. 12345678

1, Any Road
Anywhere
PO1 1PO

Minutes of a Meeting of the Board of Directors

Date of the meeting held at the Registered Office of the Company: **02/04/24**

Present:

Mr Joseph Jones (Director)
Mrs Susan Jones (Director)

DIVIDENDS

It was resolved that the company pay an interim dividend in respect of the period ending **31/12/24** to holders registered as at **02/04/24** as follows:

Share class	Dividend rate	Date to be paid
Ordinary of £1	**£100 per share**	**02/04/24**

ANY OTHER BUSINESS:

There being no further business the meeting was closed.

J Jones
....
Signed on Behalf of the Board

Name: J Jones   Date: 02/04/24   Position: Director

Notice that the amount of the dividend is expressed as so much *per share.*

7.4.2. *Sample – Dividend Confirmation*

Here is an example of a dividend confirmation. One of these must be given to each shareholder when the dividend is paid:

Property Company Limited

Company Registration No. 12345678

1, Any Road
Anytown
PO1 1PO

Dividend Confirmation

Interim dividend for the period ending 31st December 2024 to shareholders registered on 2nd April 2024

Payment Date
02/04/24

Shareholder Details
Mrs Mary Jones 1, Any Road Anytown PO1 1PO

Shareholding	Dividend rate	Dividend Payment
40 Ordinary shares of £1	**£100 per share**	**£4,000**

This confirmation should be kept as part of your financial records.

Susan Jones
……………………………………..
(director)

Date:

It may seem a nuisance putting this paperwork in place, but too many companies get themselves into trouble by not doing this properly.

7.5. Two Pitfalls to Avoid when Making Dividend Payments

Two of the commonest problems with company dividends are:

7.5.1. *"Illegal" Dividends.*

If the company pays a dividend that cannot be covered by its distributable profits, the shareholders will usually have to repay the dividend to the company, and they and the company may be taxed as if, instead of having paid them a dividend, the company had made a loan to them.

The company would also have to pay a temporary tax charge at 33.75% on the amount of the "loan", and *this* tax will be repaid to the company only once the shareholders have repaid the dividend.

(**Note:** the tax rate increased from 25% to 32.5% for amounts advanced on or after 6 April 2016, and increased again to 33.75% for loans made on or after 6 April 2022.

While this provisional tax charge is ultimately repayable by HMRC once the loan is repaid (or written off), it can be many months after the loan is made good that the tax is repayable (see also 13.4 "Loans to Participators")

7.5.2. *Timing of Dividends*

Too often, a company's shareholders simply draw the cash they need from the company, and then declare a dividend at the end of the year, that is equivalent to the cash they have taken from the company.

If this practice is discovered by HMRC, such as during an investigation of the company, the onus will be on the shareholders to prove that the cash they took out during the year was a loan from the company, which was repaid by the dividends declared after the end of the year, and **not** a disguised salary (on which, of course, PAYE and NIC will be due).

7.6. Using Dividend Waivers – An Effective Tax Planning Tool

It is possible for a shareholder to waive his or her right to a dividend.

This might be done because he has had enough income for the year, and does not want to pay tax on the dividend when he does not need the money.

Provided the following issues are carefully considered, a dividend waiver can be an effective tax planning tool.

> **Caution**
>
> Take care – dividend waivers are likely to be closely looked at by HMRC to see if they have been done properly, and there may be extra tax to pay if they are not.

A dividend cannot be waived once it has become payable, so interim dividends must be waived before they are paid, but final dividends must be waived before they are <u>declared</u>.

The waiver will take the form of a written document in which the shareholder gives up his right to the dividend. This should be in the form of a Deed, and **you may want to take advice to ensure that the paperwork is legally effective**.

The minutes of the meeting at which the dividend is paid (interim) or declared (final) should include a reference to the fact that the directors were shown a waiver of the dividend due to Mrs X, and make it clear this was done before the dividend was declared or paid.

7.7. Watch out for the "Settlements" Legislation

It is essential that the waiver cannot be attacked under the "settlements" legislation. It is easiest to explain this with an example.

Case Study - 10   "Settlements" Legislation

Before the meeting at which the dividend in Case Study - 9 is paid, Joe (who is the only 40% taxpayer) decides he does not want a dividend from the company, because he and Mary have enough other income for the year and Joe would prefer not to pay Income Tax on a dividend he does not need.

He has a Dividend Waiver drafted by his solicitor and "executes" it (this is lawyer-speak for signing it in front of a witness) then gives the Waiver to his daughter Sue, the company secretary.

The interim dividend of £100 per share is therefore paid to Mary and Sue, but not to Joe:

	Company	Mary	Joe	Sue
Distributable profits	10,000			
Dividends Paid	(6,000)	4,000	Waived	2,000
Distributable profits	4,000			

This should be acceptable to HMRC, but supposing the company decided to pay a dividend of £150 per share:

	Company	Mary	Joe	Sue
Distributable profits	10,000			
Dividends Paid	(9,000)	6,000	Waived	3,000
Distributable profits	1,000			

HMRC will argue that of that £9,000 dividend actually paid out, £3,000 should be taxed on Joe!

This may seem illogical at first, but consider what would have happened if Joe had not waived his right to a dividend, and a payment of £150 per share had been made:

	Company	Mary	Joe	Sue
Distributable profits	10,000			
Dividends Paid	(15,000)	6,000	6,000	3,000
Distributable profits	Minus 5,000, so Illegal dividend if no waiver			

In other words, the only reason why the company was able to pay Mary £6,000 and Sue £3,000, instead of £4,000 and £2,000 respectively, **was because Joe had waived his right to his dividends.**

HMRC will say that Joe has made a "settlement" of £3,000 of his income entitlement on Sue and Mary. This is a technical area of tax law, and there are arguments against HMRC's point of view – particularly in relation to the enhancement of daughter Sue's dividend – but what is certain is that using a waiver in this way is likely to lead to time-consuming and expensive enquiries from HMRC. Particular care is recommended where someone consistently waives his or her dividend entitlement for several years.

8. The Property Development Company

Much of what we have covered so far has been from the perspective of a property investor, although the basics of company law and dividends apply pretty much universally. In this chapter, will now consider some aspects specific to the property developer.

8.1. The Property Developer

A **property developer** buys property (or sometimes bare land) with the intention of improving the property (or building a new property) and selling it on in the short term, at a profit. By contrast, a property investor holds on to his or her property more for the long term, generally with an expectation of capital growth but without a short term profit motive.

> The important distinction for tax purposes is that a property developer is **trading**.

The property developer will pay Income Tax on the profits he or she makes from selling the properties, whereas the property investor will pay Capital Gains Tax if and when he sells one of his investment properties.

An individual who is trading in property will also be liable to pay National Insurance Contributions (NICs) on his profits, unless he is over the state pension age (depending on a person's exact date of birth – the qualifying age has been increased for women, to equal that of men, and then increased for both sexes to 67 and beyond).

8.2. Companies and Property Developers

This gives us a rather different picture when we compare trading as an individual property developer, with doing the same thing through a company.

> **Case Study - 11   Using a Company for Your Property Development Activities**
>
> Dave trades as a property developer through a limited company. He has £50,270 other income from pensions, so he is just on the verge of paying Tax at 40% . His company makes a profit of £60,000 for the year. If he draws out all the profits from the company as dividends plus a salary just below the NIC "threshold" (see Case Studies 5 & 6), his tax position will be:
>
> | | Company | Cash for Dave | If no company | Saving |
> |---|---|---|---|---|
> | **Profit** | 60,000 | | 60,000 | |
> | **Salary** | (9,000) | 9,000 | | |

Profit	51,000			
CT due (at 19%/26.5%)	(9,765)			
Distributable profit (dividend)	41,235	41,235		
Income tax		(17,449)	(26,054)	
NIC			(2,457)	
Cash for Dave		32,786	31,489	**1,297**

Dave has saved roughly £1,300 by running the business through a company, (before considering any additional administration costs of running the company).

If Dave had a large salary from another, unrelated employment, instead of unearned income, the position would be:

	Company	Cash for Dave	If no company	(Cost)
Profit	60,000		60,000	
Salary	(9,000)	9,000		
Income tax		(3,701)	(26,054)	
Profit	51,000			
CT due (at 19%/26.5%)	(9,765)			
Distributable profit (dividend)	41,235	41,235		
Income tax		(13,748)		
NIC			(949)*	
Cash for Dave		32,786	32,997	**(211)**

* Because Dave has a substantial salary from another job, his Class 4 self-employed NICs will be restricted to the 2% rate: he will already have paid all his main rate NICs for the tax year through Class 1 deductions.

In the first scenario, using a company has saved Dave:

- A reasonable amount of Income Tax by keeping his total taxable income *almost* completely under the £100,000 threshold at which he starts to lose his tax-free Personal Allowance via the company route; *and*

- Kept him out of mainstream NICs on his property development business

In combination, these savings more than offset the general lack of efficiency from suffering Corporation Tax first, and the "double tax charge".

In the second example, Dave has already suffered the worst of the NIC cost via his other employed income, so putting his property development business through a company saves him relatively little in NICs, so effectively costs about £1,500 more, overall.

Once again, it is clear that there may be little tax advantage in using a company if you are going to want to extract **all** the profits for your personal use. Simply put, it may depend on how much NIC you may save by incorporating the property business, compared to how much extra tax you may have to pay – first on company profits, and then on dividends to extract the net funds.

Incorporation *can* offer some savings, where it is possible to utilise the comparatively low tax rate of 8.75% that applies where dividends are taxed below the Higher Rate Threshold, which is £50,270 in 2024/25 (the bands work a little differently in Scotland, as already mentioned). However, it must be noted that the profit ranges at which substantive savings can be made, can be quite narrow:

Case Study - 12   Using a Company for Your Property Development Activities – No Other Income

Diane trades as a property developer and is contemplating the transfer of her business into a limited company. If she draws out all the profits from the company as dividends, plus a salary just below the NIC "threshold" (see Case Study 5), her tax position will be:

	Company	Cash for Diane	If no company	Saving
Profit	60,000		60,000	
Salary	(12,570)	12,570		
Deduct Employers' NICs	(479)			
Profit	46,951			

CT due (at 19%)*	(8,921)			
Distributable profit (dividend)	38,030	38,030		
Income Tax		(3,367)	(11,432)	
NIC			(2,457)	
Cash for Diane		47,233	46,111	1,122

*Any tax-adjusted profits immediately above £50,000 suffer Corporation Tax at 26.5% from April 2023 (see 4.1) and we are assuming here that Diane owns / controls no other "associated" small companies (see 4.2).

This is a modest overall tax/NIC saving, but note that running a comparison at £55,000 in net profits would realise only a £400 saving, and likewise £70,000 in profits might do little more than break even. (Diane will also have to consider any additional administration costs to running a company, as previously noted).

See the Tables in Appendix B for further details of the savings / costs of incorporation, for various profit levels.

If your strategy is to leave the profits in the company and use them to finance further development, however, having a property development company will offer similar substantial cumulative tax benefits as it does to a property investor – see section 5.1.

The above model shows quite clearly that, when comparing the corporate route to an unincorporated business model, it is essential to consider a range of taxes. Comparing Income Tax alone, the company / dividend route seems far superior – **but the dividend distribution route is available only to profits that have already been subject to Corporation Tax;** a fact that seems to escape most journalists and the occasional Chancellor.

If you are already trading as a property developer, as a sole trader or a partnership, and you feel it would be beneficial to transfer the business into a company so as to take advantage of lower effective tax rates on your profits, there is an important relief from tax you can take advantage of – **incorporation relief**. This is dealt with later in this guide (see Chapter 9).

8.3. The Construction Industry Scheme ("CIS")

An important note on the Construction Industry Scheme ("CIS")

The CIS requires property developers to deduct tax from certain payments to tradesmen, and in other cases to record amounts paid and make regular returns to HMRC of those amounts. The details of this scheme are beyond the scope of this guide, but a number of smaller property development business owners are not aware that they fall within this scheme, and as a result may face penalties for failure to operate the scheme. There is no minimum level below which the scheme does not apply to a property developer.

The CIS does **not** normally apply to buy to let **investors** unless they spend over £3million on construction within the preceding 12 months. (With the caveat that HMRC *may* try to argue that CIS applies even to property investors for the duration of a significant construction project because, in HMRC's eyes, they will have temporarily transmogrified into property developers – or at least partly so). However, CIS does apply to ALL property **developers**.

To put it another way:

- Buy-to-Let property investors generally do **not** have to worry about CIS unless they take on a significant property development or refurbishment project, but

- Property developers who pay other builders or trades as part of a development project almost certainly **will** fall within the scope of CIS

- The CIS regime applies to **all** property developers, not just to property development companies

Whether a property investor has in fact started developing property in the course of the business, so as to be considered a mainstream contractor who is 'automatically' within CIS without needing a minimum £3million annual spend on construction operations, is a complex area. See for example the contrasting cases of Thornton Heath LLP v HMRC [2018] UKFTT 0685 (TC), and Mundial Invest SA Ltd V HMRC [2006].

Further details of the CIS can be found in **"Tax Tips for Property Developers and Renovators"**, which is available through www.property-tax-portal.co.uk.

8.4. Other Considerations for Property Developers – and Occasional Developers

- Most people in business will already have heard of **Making Tax Digital**, (MTD), which requires digital record-keeping, and online submission of quarterly returns to HMRC. At the time of last writing, Making Tax Digital is 'live' only for VAT-registered business, and in relation only to their VAT records and submissions.

Ordinary BTL landlords make only supplies that are exempt, so do not generally need to worry about MTD for VAT. **After the latest re-think announced in December 2022, MTD for Income Tax is now scheduled to start as follows:**

- MTD (Income Tax) for sole traders and landlords with aggregate business income **greater than** £50,000pa will be mandated from April 2026
- MTD (Income Tax) for sole traders and landlords with aggregate business income **greater than** £30,000pa will be mandated from April 2027
- MTD (Income Tax) for sole traders and landlords with aggregate business income **lower than** £30,000pa will be subject to further review, to inform the approach of any further roll-out after April 2027
- MTD (Income Tax) for partnerships is "to be advised"

The new timetable has been drawn up to give the smallest businesses more time to prepare.

MTD for Income Tax will apply to practically all landlords (and/or property developers) in receipt of more than a very modest amount of business income. Note that individuals with several businesses have to combine their annual incomes across all trading and property letting businesses, to see if and when the above thresholds are breached.

While it is clear that the government still intends to proceed with MTD for Corporation Tax, there is as yet no firm date for implementation, except that it will definitely **not** be mandatory until at least April 2026.

Meanwhile, property developers *can* make VAT-taxable supplies, so many will already be caught by this new and potentially quite burdensome regime under MTD for VAT.

- The **VAT Domestic Reverse Charge** for construction services – where the payer or contractor has to account for the sub-contractor's VAT – was meant to apply from October 2019, but was then postponed until October 2020, and then again to 1 March 2021, due to the Coronavirus pandemic. It basically applies where CIS rules are in point, in relation to "construction operations" as defined for the purposes of CIS. However, this new regime is **unlikely** to catch most small-scale property developer businesses, acting as the "End Client" in a construction chain, unless perhaps they branch into developing for business customers – other End Clients.

- Where you pay someone to do some work for you, then you should **consider whether or not they are your employee**, in which case you should apply PAYE and NICs to their bill. This is not an issue where you hire a plasterer or electrician on an *ad hoc* basis to undertake a specific piece of work. But it can become a risk where you hire the same individual(s) for regular work on a long-term basis.

    Example:

    Doreen owns numerous rental properties but also develops properties – some to add to her portfolio and others to turn around for a profit. Where she intends to sell properties for profit, this is of course trading – and probably within the Construction Industry Scheme.

    Doreen has developed a pool of trusted tradespeople – plasterers, electricians, etc.

    For instance, Doreen will always use Rowena for electrical work if she is available. But Doreen is not Rowena's only client, and Doreen may hire Rowena for one week, or a couple of days, and then not need her for the following several weeks.

    Let's suppose that Doreen takes on a particularly large project, which will require Rowena for 6 weeks. There are several factors to consider here, but it seems unlikely that Rowena will be considered Doreen's employee, particularly if they agree a fixed fee for the project, and Rowena has to make good any mistakes at her own time and expense.

    Alternatively, let's consider Giles, who occasionally acts as labourer for Doreen. Doreen reckons that the large project will last for 8 months overall, and she will need Giles throughout. Giles will work exclusively for Doreen at an agreed weekly rate for the full working week, for the duration of the project. Again, there are many factors to consider here, but one key point is that Doreen doesn't need Giles for particular tasks or stages of the project, but simply to be available to help out as and when required. Giles may well be an employee – at least for the duration of the project – and Doreen may be required to account for PAYE and NICs (as well as a plethora of other responsibilities).

It can often be difficult for tax experts to agree whether someone is self-employed (and then potentially within CIS), or an employee who should be on the payroll. And these obligations are not limited only to building work, but to potentially any personal service provided to you in the course of your business, whatever it may be. Having said that, construction is a sector that has long been considered high-risk for "false self-employment", which is why the Construction Industry Scheme was invented in the first place – it is, in effect, "PAYE-lite".

Let's suppose that Giles actually has his own company, Giles Building Services Limited, and Doreen may contract with that company for Giles' work – in which case, Giles is an employee of Giles Building Services Limited, and Doreen is simply a client of his company, rather than Giles' employer. Historically, (and very simply), this might have been sufficient for Doreen not to worry about payroll. From April 2021, however, many private businesses that engage services from individuals through those individuals' own limited companies will have to consider whether or not the relationship is akin to that of employment and, if so, to apply PAYE and NICs anyway. This is generally referred to as the "**IR35 regime**" and this new version was rolled out to large and medium-sized companies from April 2021. Again, this is not limited just to the construction sector, strictly speaking, but it seems likely that large- and medium-sized property developers will, by the nature of their business, be much more exposed to the IR35 regime than property investors of similar scale.

- See also 12.5 – **Annual Tax on Enveloped Dwellings** (but note that it applies to companies that are property investors, as well as to property development companies).

In summary, it seems fair to say that property developers are going to be increasingly busy over the next few years, acting as unpaid tax collectors for HMRC.

9. Incorporation Relief(s)

Having established that there can be good reasons to operate a business through a limited company, there will be many businesses that are already in existence and that could be better off in a corporate wrapper, rather than being able to make the choice from day one and simply growing the business in the company. In this chapter, we shall look at a CGT relief that is potentially available when the assets of an existing business are transferred into a company that you control.

This relief is known as **Incorporation Relief**.

9.1. Transferring Assets into Your Company

If you transfer any asset you own to a company that you control, for tax purposes you will be treated as having disposed of it at its current market value, so you may well find yourself making a capital gain and paying CGT, irrespective of any proceeds you may (or may not) charge. Remember, the company that will end up owning your business is a separate legal entity (even if you own all of the shares) so you are making a disposal to another party – your company.

There are, however, two forms of tax relief that may help to solve this problem and these are detailed in the following sections.

9.1.1. Holdover Relief for Gifts of Business Assets

This applies when a person carrying on a **trade** makes a gift of an asset used for that trade, or sells it at less than its market value.

Where an asset is gifted or sold at less than its market value, a claim can be made to "hold over" the gain on the **difference between the market value of the asset, and the amount (if any) actually paid for it.**

Case Study - 13   Holdover Relief on Gift of Qualifying Business Assets

Rita owns five cottages, which she bought seven years ago with a legacy from her grandmother, and which she lets out to tourists as "furnished holiday accommodation*". This is effectively treated as a trade for CGT purposes (see **"Tax Tips for Property Developers and Renovators"** for details of how a property can qualify as "furnished holiday accommodation").

The cottages each produce a rental profit of £10,000 per year.

Rita does not intend to sell these cottages – she regards them as her "pension fund" and would like to be able to leave them to her children when she dies.

At the moment, she has a highly paid job, and does not need all the income from these cottages, so her Tax Adviser suggests that she might benefit from transferring these cottages into a company.

She bought each cottage seven years ago for £50,000, and they are now worth £150,000 each, so she would make a capital gain of £100,000 on each cottage. As these are qualifying holiday cottages, she will be eligible for Entrepreneurs' Relief (now called Business Asset Disposal Relief – see Chapter 10) and so pay CGT at only 10%. The potential CGT exposure is (£100,000 x 5 = £500,000 - £3,000 Annual Exemption = £497,000) @ 10% = £49,700.

Her Tax Adviser suggests she set up a company, and sell the cottages to it for £50,600 each, and make a claim to "hold-over" the rest of the gain.

He explains that the tax calculation will work like this:

Sale proceeds of cottages (ignore rest of the gain for now)	253,000
Less cost of cottages	(250,000)
Capital gain on sale proceeds	3,000
Annual CGT exempt amount for 2023/24	(3,000)
Taxable gains for year	NIL
CGT	NIL

The balance of the capital gain – originally £500,000 but now reduced to £497,000 because the company has paid slightly more for the cottages than their CGT cost to Rita – has been held over, and will be chargeable when the company sells or otherwise disposes of the properties.

The company does not necessarily need to pay Rita £253,000 in cash. Instead it credits her with having lent this money to the company. Rita will be able to draw this loan out of the company as and when she needs the money, and without paying any Income Tax.

Meanwhile, the company is paying only 19% Corporation Tax on the rents it receives, (in 2025, assuming the business' taxable profits do not exceed £50,000pa), instead of the 40% Income Tax Rita was paying. **On the combined rental profits of £50,000, this is a tax saving of a little over £10,000 per year**. This is a substantial saving, for so long as Rita does not need to extract the funds for personal use, and suffer tax accordingly, on the payment of salary or dividends to her.

There is one downside to this, however. For the purposes of Stamp Duty Land Tax, the properties are, again, treated as transferred to her company at their market value, and so the company will have to pay SDLT on £750,000, which will cost it £47,500, assuming the properties are transferred to the company before 31 March 2025 – 1.3 and see also Chapter 12).

Rita must decide if this up-front cost is worth paying.

Note that this strategy is specific to Rita's circumstances, and in particular to the fact that she intends to leave the holiday cottages to her children.

If instead she hoped ultimately to sell the properties, she might well do better to keep them in her personal ownership, because of the 10% rate of CGT she will pay on the gain, compared to 19%+ that the company would pay (although she *might* be able to find a buyer willing to acquire her company shares, whose sale may also qualify for Entrepreneurs' Relief, (Business Asset Disposal Relief), rather than the actual properties themselves – assuming that the favourable tax regime for Furnished Holiday Accommodation still applies at that future date).

*This special tax regime is for short-term lettings, that may or may not actually be let to holidaymakers. In the 2024 Spring Budget, it was announced that the regime would be withdrawn from April 2025 but since the announcement of the General Election, it is unclear if the withdrawal will be postponed, or even cancelled. For more on this and the possible implications, please see **"Tax Tips for Property Developers and Renovators"**

9.1.2. *Incorporation in Exchange for Shares*

There is another type of CGT relief, which applies when a business is transferred, **basically in its entirety** (or, the entirety of its assets, at least), to a company and instead of paying cash (or leaving the amount owed on loan account with the company), the company issues shares in exchange for the assets.

It works like this:

Case Study - 14   Incorporation in Exchange for Shares

Bill has a business with a market value of £100,000. If he were to sell it for that sum, he would make a capital gain of (say) £70,000. He sets up a company, and transfers the business to the company. The company does not pay him anything for the business. Instead, it issues 1,000 £1 Ordinary shares to him.

From the company's point of view, it now owns a business worth £100,000, and the "cost" of that business from the company's point of view is £100,000, being the shares it issued – so if it sold the business tomorrow, it would not make a capital gain.

From Bill's point of view, he now owns 1,000 shares worth £100 each (value of company = £100,000, divided by the 1,000 shares).

Because he qualifies for "Incorporation relief" on this transaction, he is not charged any Capital Gains Tax, but the gain he *would* have been taxed on is deducted from the "cost" of his shares for CGT purposes, so the cost of his shares is deemed to be £30 each (£100,000 - £70,000 = £30,000, divided by the 1,000 shares). This is Bill's original CGT "base cost" for his business, pre-incorporation.

The fact that the company is treated as acquiring the business at its market value offers another planning opportunity:

> **Case Study - 15   Incorporation Followed by Sale of Business**
>
> John has a trading business with a market value of £1,000,000. He wants to sell it, and use the sale proceeds to buy a portfolio of investment properties, which he sees as his "retirement fund".
>
> If he simply sold the business, he would make a capital gain of (say) £800,000, on which CGT of c£80,000 would be due, assuming he qualifies for Entrepreneurs' Relief (now Business Asset Disposal Relief).
>
> Instead, he transfers the business to a company in exchange for shares. The company issues 1,000 shares to him in exchange for the business. The position is therefore:
>
> The company now owns the business, which for capital gains purposes "cost" it £1,000,000. John has 1,000 shares worth £1,000,000, but which for CGT purposes "cost" him £200,000 (after deducting the held-over capital gain of £800,000).
>
> The company now sells the business for £1,000,000. Because its cost to the company was £1,000,000, **the company makes no gain at all and has no tax to pay**. The company can spend the whole £1,000,000 on investment properties, and John should have a more comfortable retirement than if he had sold the business himself. John may still have to pay Income Tax on any funds he draws out of the business, but he can control exactly how much he takes, and how he is taxed – such as making best use of the (still) relatively low rates applicable to dividends.

9.2. Watch Out for Some Pitfalls

The previous case study looks almost too good to be true, and like most such things, there are a number of pitfalls that one needs to be wary of.

These pitfalls include:

9.2.1.   "Preordained Series of Transactions"

There is a rule of law developed by the courts which allows HMRC to disregard a transaction if it is part of a series of transactions which were set up in advance, and the transaction in question was "inserted" simply for the purpose of avoiding tax.

In other words, HMRC might say that the reality was that John sold the business himself, and the transfer to the company was "inserted" purely for tax avoidance. For this reason, it would be most important that John had **not** started the process of selling the business directly to a third party, before he decided to transfer it to the company as an interim step.

Anyone contemplating using the same strategy as John should take advice from a Tax Adviser on whether HMRC would be likely to attack it as "preordained".

9.2.2. Stamp Duty Land Tax

As we have already seen, SDLT is charged on the market value of a property when it is transferred to one's own company, so if a substantial part of the value of John's business was in any property it/he owned, there might well be an SDLT cost to factor into the equation. Usually, John cannot simply refrain from transferring just the business property into the company – see 9.3 below.

9.2.3. What is a "Business"?

The legislation uses the word "business", but HMRC interpret the meaning of this word quite narrowly. In particular, they take the view that a property investment business may not automatically qualify as a "business" for the purposes of incorporation relief.

There have been cases where property investment businesses have been transferred to companies and managed to get incorporation relief. Where the business involves a number of properties and involves a lot of management work, it is possible that HMRC would not dispute the relief, but each case needs to be looked at on its merits, and there can be no guarantees that there will not be a challenge from HMRC (although it may be possible to get "clearance" from HMRC beforehand).

In some cases, however, it may be worthwhile taking the risk.

9.2.4. Highly-Geared Businesses

Where the gain is substantial in relation to the market value of the business (as adjusted for its liabilities on incorporation, such as loans, mortgages, etc.) then **it may not be possible to postpone all of the gain**. This will often be a potential problem where properties have repeatedly been re-mortgaged as they have increased in value, over a long period of ownership.

9.2.5. Shifting Values – IHT and CGT and Preserving Symmetry

When we talk about incorporating a business, we generally assume that –

- People will set up a "fresh" new company for this purpose – i.e., no (or negligible) pre-existing value in the business beforehand, and
- The ownership in the company will reflect the ownership in the business being incorporated.

The main reason for this is that if the proportions are not maintained, then one or more co-owners will lose out from the transfer, while others will gain, as more overall value passes.

Case Study - 16 "Asymmetrical" transfers and additional complexities

Gandalf and Rudolph, who have no connection other than by reason of being fellow partners, etc., own a property development partnership conveniently worth £1,000,000, that is held 75:25 in Gandalf's favour. They decide to incorporate the business but the shares in the fresh company are held 50:50.

If the partnership business is transferred under these ratios as they stand, then Gandalf is effectively giving away ¼ of the partnership business – his ownership of the underlying stake in the partnership assets will fall from 75% to 50%. Meanwhile the underlying value of Rudolph's interest in the partnership business assets will rise on transfer from 25% to 50%.

Both CGT and IHT are potentially in point where someone does something so that their interest in an asset is reduced. In this case, Gandalf's wealth will have fallen by £250,000 on a gift of his partnership assets to a connected company. This will leave him exposed to an IHT charge (and it cannot be *potentially exempt* from IHT, because it is not a gift to another individual – see Chapter 17).

Perhaps the easiest way to "fix" this is for Gandalf to hold 75% of the shares in the new company, prior to the transfer of partnership assets. While the shares have negligible value, then this is a straight forward matter.

Let's suppose instead that this is not a brand-new company but in fact one that is long-standing, and worth (say) £4million.

Will Rudolph be happy to gift a valuable 25% stake in the company to Gandalf, just to smooth the path of Incorporation Relief? Even if he were happy to let go of shares potentially worth as much as £1million in this alternative scenario with a well-established target company, it would likely trigger a significant capital gain for Rudolph on the shareholding he disposes of (although he may be able to qualify for CGT Gift Relief in some scenarios – see 9.1.1).

As an alternative to simply transferring shares there is an option to agree to issue more shares – but (say) only to Gandalf, while Rudolph's shareholding stays the same, thus:

> Prior to transferring the partnership business into the established company, the company issues 100 shares at par (say £1 per share) to Gandalf, so that his holding increases to 150 shares, while Rudolph sticks at 50 shares. Gandalf now holds 75% of the shares in the company, that is now effectively aligned with the corresponding interests in the partnership. This is called "value-shifting" and is again susceptible to attack via CGT anti-avoidance rules, as a deemed disposal by Rudolph to Gandalf. See also 17.8 for possible IHT implications.

Admittedly, if the parties were working on an arm's length basis, it is unlikely that Rudolph would accept either simple approach, practically speaking, as it would significantly reduce his interest in the company. For instance, in the second scenario with a valuable company, it is more likely that Rudolph would insist on the shares' being issued for a significant premium, that recognised the change in ownership and control of the company. These relatively simple examples are intended to give a sense of the "capital tax" implications – CGT and IHT – in doing so, and why real-life incorporations should be undertaken with the benefit of competent professional advice.

9.3. Comparing Incorporation and Gift Relief – Key Points

Incorporation Relief involves 'rolling' the gain into the shares. This reduces the CGT base cost of the shares, for the CGT calculation when *they* are sold. If the company sells the individual assets, it will be deemed to have acquired them at their market value on transfer-in. If, however, the shareholder sells (or otherwise disposes of) some of his shares, then a corresponding proportion of the postponed gain will be deemed, in effect, to resurface at that point (but if the company is split into a sufficiently large number of shares, and the shareholder has sufficient time, then a reasonable amount of those gains can be "washed out" by making sure to use each CGT Annual Exemption, over the coming years).

Incorporation Relief requires the **entire** business to be transferred across in exchange for the shares. Simply put, it is "all or nothing" (so, if there are problematic assets, it may be better to dispose of them separately beforehand, so long as it can be argued that there is still a qualifying business left afterwards, then to incorporate and claim relief on what remains).

Gift Relief works on an asset-by-asset basis, and it is perfectly acceptable to apply Gift Relief to some assets transferred but not others, and/or to leave some assets behind. Gift Relief 'rolls' the gain into the asset in question: if the company sells one of those assets then it will trigger the charge postponed on that particular asset. If the shareholder sells or otherwise disposes of his or her shares rather than those assets, the postponed gain remains undisturbed, in the corresponding corporate assets.

Gift Relief is available only for qualifying assets – generally assets used in a trade, such as property development. Normally, property letting businesses will not qualify for Gift Relief, although Furnished Holiday Accommodation is eligible, as a special category of letting – for so long as it remains available – see **"Tax Tips for Property Developers and Renovators"** (as are hotels and some Bed and Breakfast-type businesses, which may constitute trading activities in their own right).

9.4. Incorporating an Existing Property Investment Portfolio

Case Study - 17 Incorporating an Investment Portfolio

Jill has a business of exactly the same value as John's in Case Study - 15, but it consists of several commercial properties. She wants to sell these, and invest the money in buying an hotel.

She has been to a leading Tax Counsel, who has advised her that there is a good chance that her business would qualify for incorporation relief. He stresses that there is still a risk that it could be challenged by HMRC, however.

If Jill simply sells her properties, she will make a gain of £800,000, just like John. Her investment properties do not qualify for Entrepreneurs' Relief, however, so her CGT bill would be around £159,000 (using the new, lower, CGT rates

> applicable from April 2016 for **non**-residential property gains). If she transfers the business to a company and her incorporation relief is NOT denied by HMRC, the only cost will be the SDLT of £39,500 on the transfer of the properties to the company. (Note that, as these are not residential properties, the SDLT rate is determined at different rates to those applicable to residential properties).
>
> If the incorporation relief is denied, she will pay CGT of £159,000 but the company will still make no capital gain. It will, however, have paid the £39,500 SDLT.
>
> Jill must decide if the *possible* saving of £159,000 CGT is worth the extra cost of £39,500 SDLT. The risk can be reduced by applying for "non-statutory clearance" from HMRC, before the transaction is undertaken.

9.5. Disincorporation – an Overview of the Tax Aspects

We consider Exit Strategies in Chapter 16, but these largely assume that the reader is contemplating retiring from the business or similar.

Alternatively, a director/shareholder may want to continue with the business, but find that the corporate wrapper is becoming too expensive, against a backdrop of rising Corporation Tax rates, dividend taxation, further regulations, etc. The issue may then be how to **dis**incorporate the business so that it may be transferred out of the company, as a going concern, then to be carried on in a personal capacity by the former shareholders, going forwards.

As with incorporation, this requires careful consideration and specialist advice but in summary, the key tax issues are likely to include:

- Closing Stock will usually be transferred at market value – potentially triggering a profit in the company – although the parties can often agree to make a joint election to use a lower value

- Capital Allowances will likely trigger a Balancing Charge in the company that assumes a transfer at market value by default. But here again, a joint election may be available to fix the value at a lesser amount; the treatment for different categories of plant can become quite involved (for example, see the clawback provisions for certain assets acquired under "full expensing" at 1.1) and care will be needed to ensure that the assets are dealt with correctly and efficiently.

- Chargeable capital assets, such as plant and machinery used in the activity, premises or investment property will be disposed of to a connected party, (the individual owner(s)-to-be), so triggering a disposal deemed to be for market value – regardless of any proceeds received (or not)

- In terms of goodwill or similar intangible assets, the Corporate Intangibles regime will likely apply: the rules for intangible assets have been through several changes over the years so to summarise, there may well be a charge to Corporation Tax on deemed profits from their disposal

- Stamp Duty Land Tax (or devolved equivalent) may arise on the transfer of any land and/or buildings out of the company to the individual owner(s). It may in some cases be possible to avoid an SDLT charge depending on the method of distributing SDLT'able assets.

- VAT may be due if the company is VAT-registered, in which case the sale or transfer of the business assets would normally amount to a VAT'able supply, but the company may well be eligible to treat the disposal as a "Transfer of a Going Concern" that is outside the scope of VAT (with no VAT then due). However, note that there are several anti-avoidance criteria, particularly with land and buildings, and both the company and the new owners must follow the rules carefully to stay within the TOGC regime and avoid triggering a VAT charge.

- Assuming the company is solvent, the company will likely be formally wound up as part of the process, through a Members' Voluntary Liquidation – this may in turn be eligible for Business Assets Disposal Relief (ER/BADR – see Chapter 10 below)

Further potential complications include:

- While the distribution on a formal liquidation involving a liquidator is capital and subject to CGT, the fact that the former owners of the company are likely then to be carrying on the same business in a personal capacity means that there is a chance that "anti-phoenixing" anti-avoidance legislation will be invoked, then to treat the distribution as income, rather than capital – even retrospectively (see 16.6.3).

- Transactions in Securities – another anti-avoidance regime, that has been extended in scope specifically to cover the liquidation of a company and may also be invoked to tax something as income, that would usually be treated as subject to CGT, etc. Usually, one can approach HMRC for advance "clearance" – confirmation that HMRC will **not** invoke the TiS legislation under the circumstances as described.

- Inheritance Tax may be triggered if the ownership of the business outside of the company is not "symmetrical"/aligned with the value in the shareholdings prior to disincorporation (see 9.2.5 above for a sense of the underlying principles)

10. Entrepreneurs' Relief ("ER") from CGT – Now "Business Asset Disposal Relief" – and Investors' Relief

ER was introduced for gains made after 5 April 2008, and replaced the old "Taper Relief" as applied to qualifying business assets. The 2020 Budget contained provisions for it to be renamed as "Business Asset Disposal Relief" ("BADR"). The new "BAD Relief" is essentially the old ER but with a reduced lifetime allowance.

Under ER, there was a cumulative lifetime allowance of £10,000,000, applicable to gains on one or more disposals of qualifying business assets, either together or over the years. Instead of being charged at the more common 20%, the first £10 million of such gains were charged to tax at 10%. For disposals made on or after 11 March 2020 under the new BADR title, that lifetime limit has been reduced to £1,000,000.

"Business Assets" are strictly defined for ER/BADR purposes – the following is a basic summary of the qualifying circumstances:

- A disposal of a sole trading business held for at least 2 years, or an interest likewise held in a partnership, provided it is a trading business and not an investment business

- A disposal of "part of a business" – this has to be an identifiable part of the business, not just an asset used in the business, so for example, a farmer could not claim ER/BADR on the sale of a few of his fields, but he might if he sold his pasture, milking parlour, and dairy herd, while keeping his arable land – that would be a sale of a "part" of his business (the dairying part).

- An associated sale of assets used in the business, alongside the disposal of a substantive interest in, or (at least partly) retiring from, or ceasing the business.

- A sale of shares in a trading company, provided the shareholder was an employee or a director of the company, AND had held at least 5% of the voting shares and income/capital rights for at least two years before the sale.

There is now a separate form of relief available for long-term investors in eligible trading companies. This Investors' Relief allows 'external' investors, who are not otherwise involved in the business, to benefit from the 10% rate, provided they subscribe for new shares and hold on to them for at least 3 years from 6 April 2016.

Note that ER/BADR is available to trading businesses such as property development businesses, but not generally to investment businesses such as property letting activities.

Where a business has both trading and investment activities, then ER/BADR will potentially still be available so long as the investment proportion is not "substantial" (generally taken by HMRC to be more than 20% of the overall business, although how they will manage following the Upper Tribunal hearing in **Allam v HMRC [2021] UKUT 0291 (TCC)** remains to be seen).

The detailed rules for Entrepreneurs' Relief/Business Asset Disposal Relief and the new Investors' Relief are complicated, and you should consult a Tax Adviser if you think you might qualify for either, on a sale/disposal that you are contemplating.

The rules have been repeatedly tweaked in the last few years. For example, the qualifying assets now need to have been held for at least two years, broadly for any disposal on or after 6 April 2019, whereas prior to that, the minimum holding period was just one year. See also Profits from Dealing In or Developing UK Land ("Transactions in Land") below.

11. Reinvestment Relief

In this chapter we will look at "Reinvestment Relief". Numerous questions are asked about this relief and we will try to get to grips with the most common scenarios when this relief may be considered.

11.1. Property Investors and Reinvestment Relief

Property investors often ask if they can defer paying CGT on gains they have made by reinvesting the money in another property.

Unfortunately, this is generally not possible.

There are only two exceptions:

11.1.1. Business Assets

A company (or an individual or partnership) which is carrying on a trade can claim "rollover relief" from tax on its capital gains if it sells an asset it has used for its trade and spends all the sale **proceeds** on buying another asset to use in its trade. Those sale proceeds do not need to be "ring fenced" or identified separately and it is sufficient merely to apply an equivalent amount of funds to make a qualifying purchase within the relevant time limits. Partial reinvestment of the proceeds may secure partial relief – see below.

Generally, the new asset must Cbe purchased within the period that begins one year before the old asset is sold, and ends three years after that sale.

There are several categories of asset that qualify for this relief, and among them are land and buildings that are occupied and used for the purposes of the trade being carried on.

While land and buildings may qualify for the relief, note that:

- The relief will **not** apply to a buy-to-let investor, because they are *investing*, not trading, and the relief is available only to *trading* activities; and

- While a property developer is trading and may well be eligible in some scenarios, property bought for development is broadly *stock in trade*, (subject to Income Tax), rather than a fixed or *capital* asset, (subject to CGT), and scope for land and buildings will be restricted to their own offices, yards or similar.

11.1.2. Furnished Holiday Lettings

These are a special category of buy to let property – see Case Study - 13 – and rollover relief is available if one of these specially eligible properties is sold and the proceeds used to buy another eligible property.

Note that the Government announced at Spring Budget 2024 that it intended for the favourable environment for qualifying Furnished Holiday Lettings would be abolished with effect from April 2025 (although it remains to be seen whether – or to what extent – this will be affected by the General Election). See also "**Tax Tips for Property Developers & Renovators**".

For so long as furnished holiday accommodation is still around to qualify for reinvestment relief, note that there is a quirk in the rules, to cater for the regime permitting CGT-free disposals of one's only or main residence.

Because it would be possible for a person to roll a gain on an old holiday cottage over into a new one, and then move into it as his or her main residence and so "exempt" the entire gain from CGT on *that* cottage's later disposal, the relief is only given provisionally and if, when the new property is sold, it qualifies for relief from CGT as a main residence, the gain previously held over is brought back into charge.

11.1.3.   Reinvestment Relief - Example

Case Study - 18   Property Development and Reinvestment Relief

Chris owns a property development company, ChrisCo., that owns its commercial offices, from which the trading activity is carried on. The offices cost £50,000 six years ago, and he sells them for £200,000, because he needs larger premises.

The gain of £150,000 will **not** qualify for ER/BADR because it is simply an asset used in the company's trade, so it has a taxable gain of £150,000, on which the company would likely pay £37,500 at the main 25% tax rate.

ChrisCo. had already spent £220,000 on another office building six months prior to the sale of the old one (and this is why the qualifying period for re-investment actually starts *before* the disposal that gives rise to the gain: sometimes you have to secure the replacement asset before you can sell the "old" asset). The company has effectively used the entire amount of the sale proceeds from the old offices to buy the new building, so all of the capital gain on the old premises may instead be "rolled over" into the new one, and ChrisCo makes a claim for Reinvestment Relief.

When ChrisCo. comes to sell the new office building, its cost for the purposes of CGT* will be reduced by the amount of the gain that has been rolled over into it:

Amount spent on new office building	220,000
Less capital gain rolled over from old premises	(150,000)
Cost of new office building for CGT purposes	70,000

> There is some relief even if you do not reinvest all of the sale proceeds. Suppose that the new premises costs ChrisCo. only £180,000. This is less than the sale proceeds of the old office, so the computation goes like this:
>
> First, find the amount of the sale proceeds not reinvested. Here, this is £20,000 (£200,000 - £180,000). This is less than the capital gain of £150,000 on the old building, so the amount of the gain that has not been reinvested is £20,000.
>
> ChrisCo. will remain taxable on a gain of £20,000, and the cost for CGT purposes of the new office building, for when *it* comes to be sold, will be:
>
> | | |
> |---|---|
> | **Amount spent on new office building** | 180,000 |
> | **Less capital gain rolled over from old premises** | (130,000) |
> | **Cost of new office building for CGT purposes** | 50,000 |
>
> *Strictly speaking, a company does not pay CGT, but Corporation Tax on capital gains. There are no separate rates for CGT in a company – see 4.1 above.

Reinvestment Relief includes a number of criteria for a successful claim, but there are also several special easements that may help in certain cases, including:There is another way to defer a capital gain by reinvesting into specially qualifying companies, rather than into property itself. This is by using the **Enterprise Investment Scheme ("EIS")** for individuals. This is a scheme that offers tax advantages for investment in the appropriate sort of company.

11.2. Deferring Capital Gains by Reinvesting

11.2.1.   Enterprise Investment Scheme (EIS)

The **EIS** offers three forms of tax relief to an individual who invests in **new** shares – a subscription – in an EIS company:

- Income Tax relief (currently at 30%) on the amount (generally up to £1,000,000 but the limit has increased to £2million for "knowledge-intensive company" share investments from 6 April 2018) invested in EIS qualifying shares, provided that the individual is not "connected" with the company – that is, he and his "associates" do not own or control more than 30% of it.

- If the shares qualify for the above Income Tax relief, and they are later sold at a loss, that adjusted loss can be deducted from the investor's income for the year.

- If the shares qualify for the Income Tax relief, and are sold at a profit (gain) after more than three years, the profit is exempt from CGT, except for any gains "deferred" – see next bullet point.

- Deferral of *other* capital gains on **any amount** reinvested in EIS shares – this relief applies whether or not the individual is "connected" to the EIS company, and is the one we shall concentrate on here.

    The investment must be made within the same time limit as for rollover relief – one year before to three years after the gain to be deferred.

An EIS company must meet certain conditions if it is to be a "qualifying company" and its shareholders can get tax relief on their investment.

The detailed rules are very complicated, and expert tax advice is essential if you are contemplating an EIS investment, but in outline:

- The company must not be listed on a Stock Market
- It must not be controlled by another company
- It must carry on a "qualifying trade" and have a "permanent establishment" in the UK

A qualifying trade is defined by excluding certain types of trade – any other trade will be a "qualifying trade".

The following are **"excluded activities"** and a company which carries on any of these trades will **not** be a "qualifying company" for EIS purposes:

- Dealing in land, commodities, shares or other financial instruments
- Dealing in goods (except for ordinary wholesalers and retailers)
- Banking, insurance, money-lending, and other financial activities
- Leasing or receiving royalties or licence fees
- Providing legal or accountancy services
- **Property development** (before you get any ideas..!)
- Farming or market gardening
- Woodlands or forestry activities
- Shipbuilding
- Producing coal or steel
- Running hotels or similar establishments

- Running nursing homes or residential care homes
- Subsidised electricity generation

The EIS company must carry on its qualifying trade for at least three years from the date it issues the EIS shares on which tax relief is claimed.

The list of "excluded activities" means that a property company could never be an EIS company, but an EIS company investment in a different field may nevertheless be of interest to a property investor who has already made a large capital gain by selling one or more of his properties.

Case Study - 19   EIS Deferral Relief

Gary has just sold his property portfolio for £2 million, and has made a gain of £500,000.

He decides to set up an eligible trading company. His Tax Adviser explains that it should be possible to set the company up in such a way that he will qualify for EIS deferral relief.

Gary pays his new company £500,000 and the company issues shares to him in return. Because Gary owns more than 30% of the company (in fact, he owns it all!) he cannot claim the EIS Income Tax relief on his subscription for the shares, but he can still claim deferral relief for his capital gain.

As Gary has invested the full amount of the gain in the EIS company, all of his capital gain is deferred – **note that for the EIS it is not necessary to invest all the sale proceeds, (unlike with rollover relief above), but just the gain itself.**

The company spends the £500,000 on setting up a trade (it must do this within strict time limits). Provided it continues to run the trade for at least three years, Gary's deferral relief is safe.

When Gary sells the shares, the £500,000 gain he deferred becomes taxable again – though he could defer the gain once more by investing in another EIS company.

Any gain on the shares themselves will not be exempt (because he did not qualify for the Income Tax relief as he owned over 30% of the company), but this too could be deferred by another EIS investment.

Finally, while the opportunities for formal reinvestment relief may be limited, note that Case Study 15 illustrates a possible mechanism to achieve something similar, when incorporating an eligible property business. There is also a miniature version of EIS, called the "Seed Enterprise Investment Scheme", but it is aimed at very small businesses and may be of little use for substantial property gains.

12. Some Property Tax Pitfalls

In this chapter we will look at one or two pitfalls that the property business owner should be aware of.

12.1. Partnerships?

We have already seen in section 2.2 of this guide that a partnership is "persons carrying on a business in common and with a view of profit".

The Partnership Act 1890 defines a "business" as including "every trade, occupation or profession".

HMRC takes the view that simply owning a property jointly with another person and receiving a share of the rent from it does not amount to an "occupation or profession", and we have already seen that it is not a trade.

They argue that in most cases, income from jointly owned property is **not** income from a partnership. (For further information on whether a co-owned property letting business is operating merely as a joint investment activity or as a 'proper' partnership, please see our separate report, "Taxation of Property Partnerships and Joint Ownership").

12.1.1. Why Does It Matter?

Given that HMRC accepts that joint owners of property can generally agree how the income from the property is divided between them, this distinction may not seem very important.

But there may be scenarios where:

- Holding some property in business partnership alongside some separate property not in partnership may prove unhelpful; but also,

- Where property is held in joint names between spouses or civil partners, where their **not** being in partnership may prove quite inflexible

In other words, *pros* and *cons*.

In the case of joint owners of property who are not married, the distinction is unlikely to become relevant unless one of them is also a partner in a trading business which itself lets property, and then only if there are losses involved:

Case Study - 20   Partnerships or not (1)

Peter is a partner in a firm of tax advisers. The firm also owns a couple of investment properties, which it lets out. For the tax year 2024/25, the rentals from these properties produce a loss, of which Peter's share is £1,000.

> Peter also owns a rental property jointly with his brother. During the same tax year, they make a profit on the rent from the property of £1,000 each.
>
> Peter cannot set the loss from the partnership rents against the profit on the jointly owned property, because they are two separate property businesses, owned in different legal "capacities" – one as a joint owner, the other as a partner.
>
> If Peter also owned another property on his own or jointly with someone else – his sister, for example – then his part of any losses on that other property/ies *could* be offset against the profit on the property owned jointly with his brother, just as if he held the property solely in his name. The key distinction is that rental profits or losses arising to a *partnership* are not the same as those arising personally or from *jointly-held property*, and must be streamed separately. In Peter's case, there is a trading partnership of tax advisors, which also holds investment properties.

Bigger problems can arise, however, with rental properties owned in joint names by a married couple (or a civil partnership).

This is because there is specific legislation (ITA 2007 s 836/7) that allocates the income from assets held in joint names between spouses and civil partners, as follows:

- The income is deemed to be split equally between the couple, UNLESS

- They do **not** in fact own equal shares of it, AND they elect (using a "Form 17")

- To be taxed based on their ACTUAL ownership of it.

Case Study - 21   Partnerships or not (2)

> Rowley and his wife Nellie own a rental property in joint names. Rowley pays Income Tax at 40%, but Nellie does not have any income. The rental profit from the property is £12,000 per year.
>
> It seems sensible to the couple (who believe, wrongly, that they are a property letting partnership), to agree that the profits of the partnership should be split 10% to Rowley, and 90% to Nellie.
>
> The tax inspector explains to them that in his opinion their property letting is not a partnership, because it does not involve sufficient business activity on their part – it is essentially a passive investment.
>
> After some argument, they reluctantly accept his view, but Nellie asks why it is so important, given that HMRC accept that joint owners can agree how to divide the income from their property.
>
> The inspector explains that this does not apply to married couples, and runs through the rules referred to above. Because the income from the jointly owned property must be split equally between them, the result is:

	Rowley	Nellie	Total
Rental split as "partnership"	1,200	10,800	12,000
Tax due	480	nil	480
Rental split 50:50	6,000	6,000	12,000
Tax due	2,400	nil	2,400

As a result of splitting the income in the correct way, the couple are paying £1,920 more Income Tax.

What could they do?

For the future, they could change their ownership of the property, by converting their ownership in joint names into a "tenancy in common" (a simple legal procedure), and Rowley could then give 4/5 of his half share to Nellie (there is no CGT on gifts between spouses – but see 12.2 next).

They would then beneficially own the property in a 90:10 proportion, and they could then submit a Form 17 to the inspector, although the new split of the income would apply only from the date they made this "declaration". Furthermore, they still do not have the flexibility of co-owners who are not married to each other / in a civil partnership: if they want to change their income split again, they will have to change the underlying beneficial ownership again.

Again, *if they were operating in a business partnership*, then they could split the profits unequally, even though they are in a married couple or civil partnership, without having to adjust their actual respective ownership in the property. It is the fact that they are 'merely' investors in joint names in a passive investment activity that restricts their flexibility in sharing rental profits between themselves as a married couple, etc.

The question of whether or not a business is being carried on in partnership or as 'mere' joint investors also has implications for SDLT in some circumstances – see later in this chapter.

12.2. SDLT Implications of Transfers Involving A Mortgage

Note that if there is a mortgage on the property, then a gift may give rise to a charge to Stamp Duty Land Tax (SDLT) and, even if it does not, the gift will generally need to be notified to HMRC on Form SDLT1. SDLT law treats the donee's accepting responsibility for the mortgage as a form of valuable consideration, chargeable to SDLT. Note that the mortgage-lender's contract may insist on any new/joint owner also taking on responsibility for the mortgage.

> **Case Study - 22   Gifts and Stamp Duty**
>
> Sam owns a buy to let property valued at £300,000, on which she has secured a mortgage of £240,000. She makes a gift of the entire property (still encumbered with the mortgage), to her wife, Georgie. The gift will escape CGT because it is a transfer between spouses / civil partners who are living together as a couple.
>
> As regards SDLT, although Georgie did not pay anything for the property, she *did* take on responsibility for the £240,000 mortgage, so she must pay SDLT of £7,200 including the 3% "additional dwelling" charge. Note that with the new regime introduced in April 2016, a married couple may have only one 'exempt main residence' between them. This is a significant increase on the pre-April 2016 rates, where the cost would have been as little as £2,300.
>
> If instead Sam had given Georgie only a half share in the property, Georgie would sometimes be treated as having taken over half the mortgage, being £120,000. This would now cost £3,600 in SDLT, but before April 2016 it would have been SDLT-free, although there would still have been a duty to notify HMRC using Form SDLT1.

12.3. SDLT, Partnerships And Incorporation

Most readers will be aware that any residential property purchase by a company will generally trigger the 3% "additional dwelling surcharge", because companies cannot themselves have a main residence. However, there is also a possible charge to SDLT on the incorporation of a property business – and it is potentially very large, since it applies to the market value of the property/ies. It doesn't matter if the company pays nothing for the portfolio, because the trigger is simply a transfer between individuals and a company with which they are "connected" – basically, in which they are shareholders.

As regards residential properties, the SDLT rate can be as high as 15%, although companies will typically be allowed to use the cheaper commercial (non-residential) property rates, when acquiring 6 or more dwellings in one contract (for those readers familiar with Multiple Dwellings Relief, note *that* Relief route was blocked for transactions effective on or after 1 June 2024, following the 2024 Spring Budget).

Partnerships (and Limited Liability Partnerships) *may* be able to avoid an SDLT charge entirely, however, thanks to specific provisions that reduce the charge when such bodies incorporate. Simple joint investments are ineligible – it cannot be a passive investment but rather an active partnership business. Businesses that think they may be eligible for partnership treatment should take detailed advice on the matter beforehand, as property businesses are liable to challenge over whether or not they actually 'qualify' as a partnership, instead of a simple joint investment, as noted above at 12.1.

Individuals should also beware creating a partnership (or LLP) in order to try to circumvent the SDLT charge on subsequent incorporation of the new partnership: there is SDLT anti-avoidance legislation that will "ignore" a series of transactions or arrangements that (loosely) are undertaken to secure a lower SDLT charge.

Even where there is a "genuine" partnership, care is needed. For example, a charge to SDLT can arise to property investment partnerships where the partners change their profit-sharing ratios. It would be rather unfortunate to have succeeded in convincing HMRC that the property letting business was in fact a genuine partnership rather than merely joint letting, only then for HMRC to enquire as to whether or not the partnership had ever changed its profit-sharing ratio…

12.4. Increased SDLT Risk For Companies – Indecision Costs Money!

Where a company purchases a single dwelling property costing more than £500,000, then it is **potentially** exposed to a 15% SDLT rate on the whole consideration, **unless** the company is to use it for:

- A property rental business, or
- A property development business

(Certain other dwellings are excluded, such as farmhouses and properties either used by employees or made available to the public).

This means that BTL landlords and property developers operating through companies should be safe from the increased SDLT charge, but perhaps one thing you should NOT say to your conveyancing solicitor when he asks what your company intends to do with the new £500,000+ residential property it has just purchased is "I don't know / I haven't decided yet"!

With regard to the 3% SDLT surcharge on additional residential properties, the maximum SDLT rate is not 15%+3% but only 15% (but note that the new 2% 'surcharge' for non-UK-resident buyers *can* increase the ceiling for the SDLT rate, in this case up to 17% - see 12.6.2). Given that companies cannot have a main residence that they can replace in order to avoid the 3% charge, it will generally fall due on **every** property purchase, including the first. However, there are measures that companies (and other property buyers) can employ to reduce their SDLT exposure when acquiring several residential properties together, such as:

- Acquiring properties that have a "mixed use", or that are not wholly used as a dwelling (for example a shop with flats above, purchased as a single unit), or
- The lower non-residential/commercial property SDLT rates when acquiring 6 or more residences together

- but note that HMRC is very likely to challenge claims that a purchase has mixed use, where it espies predominantly residential property. For example:

- Suterwalla v HMRC [2023] UKFTT 450 (TC) was found to be eligible for mixed use treatment based on a dwelling plus a separate paddock that was already subject to a grazing lease at the point of purchase; however

- Modha v HMRC [2023] UKFTT 00783 (TC) involved a quite informal grazing arrangement that was formalised after the date of purchase, and was held **not** to comprise a mixed-use acquisition for SDLT purposes

12.5. Annual Tax On "Enveloped Dwellings" (ATED)

Just in case a potential 15% SDLT charge on acquisition were not enough, there is also an Annual Tax on Enveloped Dwellings. "Enveloped Dwellings" basically means dwellings that are owned or partly-owned by a company, or similar arrangement. ATED applies only to high-value dwellings that are **individually** worth more than £500,000. Here again, relief is available from ATED for dwellings that are used in:

- A property rental business, or
- A property development business.

But relief from ATED must be claimed, so property companies have to submit a Relief Declaration Return covering their let properties, (and/) or a different Relief Declaration Return covering development properties. The deadline is usually 30 April every year, but it may be a different date for the first period in which the company has to claim the relief. There are penalties if the claims are submitted late.

Ordinary BTL properties will count as "dwellings" but hotels, guest houses, care homes and student halls of residence should not.

One or two aspects of ATED to catch out the unwary:

- ATED is assessed by reference to the dwelling's value. Where recently acquired, the cost can be used for its value. However, properties have to be revalued periodically – up until fairly recently, April 2017 *was* the most recent valuation date, with April 2022 being the next – properties may have been caught since 2023/24 that were previously 'safe'.

- If a property is let to a person "connected" with the owner(s), such as to a relative of the company's shareholder(s), then ATED is chargeable: **even if the arrangements are by way of a normal rental agreement at a full market rate, the rental business relief (or, if relevant, the property development business relief) is not available**. (See also a similar trap at 13.5 for Close Investment Holding Companies – CIHCs)

- If a high-value property is unused but is not being marketed or repaired, etc., then there is a risk that ATED will be triggered because it will fall outside the aforementioned reliefs, if only until it is active again.

- Previously, when the property was sold or there was otherwise a disposal for CGT purposes, then the company would have been subject to a special ATED-based CGT charge if it was caught by the Annual Tax itself during the time it was owned. (A corresponding proportion of the gain arising was subject to ATED CGT). The rate for ATED CGT was 28% - even though ordinary corporate capital gains are taxed at the standard rates of 19%-25%. See also Foreign Ownership, below, but note that ATED-based CGT was abolished for disposals from 2019/20 onwards (although the annual tax charge itself still remains) because the scope of 'normal' UK CGT for non-residents has widened significantly.

The rules for ATED are complex, and people new to the regime should seek advice from a suitably qualified Tax Adviser. An ordinary BTL or property development company has little to fear from ATED, however, so long as it:

- Files its Relief Declaration Return(s) on time, as and when they are required.

- Does not let connected individuals occupy its high-value properties.
- Monitors its void periods to ensure that high-value properties are actively managed in the business, and
- Monitors properties that were just under the high-value threshold when introduced but may since have increased in value.

12.6. Foreign Ownership

I have come across a number of property investors who think that holding UK property through an offshore vehicle – and/or perhaps becoming non-resident themselves – will somehow reduce their tax bill. While tax saving is not impossible, there are numerous aspects to consider, including the following:

If the individual and/or the company is not resident in the UK, then they are likely resident in another country / territory, and therefore subject to that territory's tax regime. Some territories do not tax the overseas income or gains of their residents, but most do – and some will tax more heavily than in the UK.

The UK's domestic tax code generally makes income from UK property taxable in the UK. Where they apply, Double Taxation Treaties with other countries may potentially override that rule but in fact, many Treaties actually do the opposite, and effectively allow **both** the territory where the property is located, **and** the territory where the taxpayer is resident, to tax the same property income. (Even so, either the Treaty itself, or the domestic UK tax code, will generally allow relief to avoid tax being paid twice on that income source, so this may not actually cost more tax).

A similar approach applies to an individual who is not resident in the UK but operates (say) a property development trade in the UK: the UK would still want to tax profits arising from the UK trading activity, as would, in all likelihood, the territory in which the individual was tax resident (subject to offset / deduction for overseas tax paid, as with rental profits). Furthermore, capital gains on any assets sold in the UK that were used in a UK trading activity would be subject to UK CGT, by default.

If the company's directors would prefer to remain UK-resident, note that it is quite difficult to 'keep' an offshore company offshore, if its directors are resident in the UK: if it is effectively managed in the UK then it may become UK tax resident even if originally constituted offshore. Can UK-based directors practically undertake their executive meetings and decisions offshore – and how expensive might that be?

12.6.1. *UK Capital Gains by Non-Residents*

If a non-resident individual or company sells UK **residential** property, then it will have been exposed to Non-Resident CGT (NRCGT) on the part of the gain deemed to arise since 5 April 2015, when the new regime was introduced. (There are exceptions for the main residence). NRCGT applies at the standard rates.

From 6 April 2019, the scope of the NRCGT regime was effectively widened to catch disposals of **any** UK land or property, so commercial property disposals are now caught as well. (The legislation has been comprehensively reworked so that, for example, non-resident companies strictly pay Corporation Tax on UK capital gains, rather than NRCGT, but we shall continue to use "NRCGT" in relation to individuals and companies, for simplicity).

Prior to April 2019, a non-resident company could potentially be caught for ATED CGT (see above) *and* NRCGT on the same UK residential property gain, in which case ATED CGT would take precedence (at the higher rate of 28%). ATED CGT has now been abolished.

Even if no NRCGT is due, an NRCGT return should still be filed within 60 days of conveyance, or penalties may be incurred (it was a 30-day window before 27 October 2021). Where a property has been owned for a long time, however, the relatively new NRCGT regime may **not** turn out to be that expensive.

Case Study - 23   Non Resident CGT

Jean, who is resident in France, holds a UK residential rental property in a French company, JeanCo, which it has owned since April 2003, at a cost of £250,000. It was worth £550,000 when the new NRCGT regime was introduced in April 2015, and the company sold it for £650,000 in April 2025 – i.e., twenty-two years later.

	Default Calculation	**Time-apportioned Calculation**
Proceeds April 2025	650,000	650,000
Less: Value April 2015	(550,000)	
Less: Original Cost April 2003		(250,000)
Overall Gain	**100,000**	400,000
Proportion since April 2015 10 years since April 2015 22 years' total ownership period		**182,000**
Use default calculation as lower gain	**100,000**	

There are several possible calculation methods available to JeanCo. The simplest – and default – approach is to set the proceeds against the property's value when the regime was introduced for such residential properties, on 6 April 2015.

Alternatively, it can calculate the gain over the entire ownership period (starting since March 1982, if owned earlier than that) and tax the proportion of the resulting gain attributable to the period of ownership after April 2015. In this case, the default method results in a lower gain so Jean chooses the default basis.

If JeanCo had owned the property for a longer period before the start date for residential property NRCGT, then the proportion of gain attributable to post-April 2015 on a time basis could fall to a lower amount than that derived from the default

> basis, so JeanCo might plump for the time-apportionment basis. Or, if the 2015 value were much lower, then the gain on the default approach might then be higher than that calculated on a time-apportioned basis. (There is a further alternative approach, using original cost, but it is rarely likely to be useful, except where capital losses are in point).
>
> The NRCGT regime for commercial properties, etc., is calculated in a similar way, but using the April 2019 value for comparison, rather than April 2015.
>
> **Remember that JeanCo may also be taxed in France on this gain!**

The rules capturing UK land and property gains made by non-resident entities are comprehensive and will now catch even the disposal of shares in a "property-rich" company, that derives most of its value from UK land – simply put, in some circumstances you don't even have to sell the UK property interest itself to trigger a UK tax charge, but merely the shares in the company that owns the UK land. There are safeguards for persons with small shareholdings and for companies whose ownership of UK land is incidental to their business, but the rules are complex and advice is strongly recommended.

12.6.2. SDLT Surcharge for Non-Resident Investors

Finance Act 2021 confirmed that foreign or non-UK-resident buyers acquiring residential property in England and Northern Ireland from 1 April 2021 would suffer an additional 2% SDLT charge on their acquisitions – this surcharge applies to take the maximum overall rate of SDLT payable up to as high as 17% (i.e., 15%+2%).

- Resident status does not follow the statutory residence test, but as devised for SDLT
- It generally applies where **any** of the buyers is not UK resident
- But there are relieving provisions to deal with acquisitions by spouses and civil partners where one spouse, etc., is UK-resident and the other is not
- It will apply in many cases to purchases of UK residential property by a company that has non-resident owners

12.7. International Tax Co-Operation

It is possible that some of those intending to operate their business from offshore, think that this will make it easier to conceal their business activities. HMRC and around 100 other countries' tax authorities participate in "Mutual Administrative Assistance in Tax Matters", which broadly means that:

- Other subscribing territories exchange information on taxpayers with HMRC and vice versa

- Other subscribing territories will assist HMRC in collecting tax debts that HMRC says are owed to the UK (and vice versa)

HMRC has a special penalty regime where there has been tax loss involving offshore activity, where the penalty charged can be as high as 200% of the tax due. Unsurprisingly, the highest penalty rates apply to territories where information exchange, etc., is poor.

Failing to account for UK tax on offshore income and gains can also trigger a special "strict liability" criminal offence – in this context "strict liability" means that HMRC does not have to worry about whether the taxpayer knew that he or she had done something wrong. In other words – and unusually for criminal offences – innocence is no excuse, and HMRC simply has to prove that the tax loss arose. Here again, the government is aiming at territories where information exchange, etc., is poor.

Offshore taxation can be extremely complex, because it has the potential to involve not just the UK tax regime but another country's tax code as well. It demands comprehensive advice from a specialist Tax Adviser.

There is a great deal of anti-avoidance legislation designed to attribute income or gains in an offshore company to its UK shareholders. Recently, new rules have been introduced, basically to ensure that income derived from developing UK land or property is taxed as a trade in the UK, even if the entity that owns the property has no presence in the UK whatsoever. Typically of anti-avoidance legislation, it is complex. Also typically of anti-avoidance legislation, it has far-reaching consequences for scenarios beyond the mischief it was ostensibly designed to counteract (see next). We shall look at this regime from the perspective of a UK-resident property business, on the basis that it will likely apply mostly to such domestic taxpayers anyway.

12.8. Using Companies for Specific Development Opportunities: Profits from Dealing In or Developing UK Land ("Transactions in Land")

The latest version of this regime was introduced in 2016. It was *supposed* to ensure that non-resident entities trading in UK land and property were taxed alongside their UK-based competitors. But the new regime does **not** apply *only* to non-resident companies, etc. – an oversight so obvious, it cannot but have been deliberate. In fact, the new regime quite possibly affects more UK-based businesses than overseas entities. Its introduction significantly strengthened HMRC's hand when dealing with UK businesses – again, probably not a coincidence.

The regime basically says that when you decide to develop land or property in the UK to make a profit, it is taxed as a trading endeavour. This is particularly relevant to property investors who may have held investment property for many years, and who then decide to develop the land / buildings to enhance re-sale value. In the past, property investors might have argued that they were merely enhancing a capital asset, and that the eventual sale should remain subject to CGT throughout the period of ownership. In the past, HMRC used to argue – not always successfully – that the decision to develop the land or property for re-sale had caused a "supervening trade" to spontaneously materialise, so as to over-ride the usual CGT approach. HMRC used a similar argument for "slice of the action" arrangements where a third party would offer to develop a landlord's property, and pay for the property by allocating a share in the proceeds when the development was ultimately sold on.

Simplistically, the new regime means that HMRC pretty much always wins, and developing land or property held as an investment will always be taxed as trading profits, when the development is for re-sale. This may make little difference to a company, which is taxed at the same rate for trading profits as it is for capital gains. However, it will make a very substantial difference to unincorporated property investors, who might expect to pay CGT at only 20% on a commercial property disposal, but then find that Income Tax and potentially even NICs are due at an aggregate rate of 42% or more, after developing the property for sale.

Case Study:

Yasmin is a landlady and she owns a single large block of 8 flats, which keep her very busy. Over time, the flats are getting harder to let because they are "too large" for the prevailing market. She realises that she could develop the property into practically double the number of apartments, and sell them for a substantial return. In April 2024, she decides to press ahead with the development.

She bought the property for £400,000 and at May 2024 it is worth £700,000. But at a further development cost of £200,000, she could sell the new apartments for £1,200,000 – making a further £300,000 net.

If Yasmin were to undertake the development personally, then the Transactions in Land regime would potentially catch the development phase, even if HMRC does not argue that Yasmin has embarked on a supervening trade. The point at which Yasmin decides to develop the asset for resale is when the clock stops for CGT purposes: up to that point, any increase in value since acquisition should remain subject to CGT:

	Total	Income Tax	CGT
Sale Proceeds (say) Jan 2025	1,200,000		
Less: Value when development phase commenced	(700,000)		700,000
Gives: Gross Trading Income		500,000	
Further Development Costs		(200,000)	
Trading Profit Jan 2025		300,000	
Less: Original Cost			(400,000)
Capital Gain to May 2024			300,000
Tax thereon (24%)		121,203	71,280
Residue to Yasmin net of IT / CGT			807,517

Despite making the same profit on the development phase as the original gain at April May 2024, the Income Tax cost is practically 70% higher than the corresponding CGT – an extra c£50,000. The total tax cost is nearly £200,000.

Would Yasmin be better off incorporating, and then running the development phase through her own company? If the company paid Yasmin a "slice of the action" fee for her block of flats, just as a third party developer might, then that receipt would still be treated as her trading income under the Transactions in Land" rules. But *if* Yasmin were able to claim Incorporation Relief in April 2023 to postpone the capital gain on transferring the asset to her company, (see 9.1.2), and then Entrepreneurs' Relief/Business Asset Disposal Relief on liquidating her company, (see Chapter 10), rather than taking a payment or fee from the company, then the tax costs would be:

	Default Calculation	Time-apportioned Calculation
Cumulative Sales to March 2026		1,200,000
Less: Cost of Sales -		
Property on transfer in	700,000	
Further Development Costs	200,000	
		(900,000)
Trading Profit in Company		300,000
Corporation Tax (25%)		(75,000)
Residue in Company (Sales less development costs and CT)		925,000
Yasmin: Distribution in Liquidation		925,000
Base Cost net of postponed gain		(400,000)
Annual Exemption		(3,000)
Taxable		522,000
Entrepreneurs' Relief (BADR) Rate (10%)		(52,200)
Net residue to Yasmin		**872,800**

This route appears to serve Yasmin rather better than managing everything personally, or adopting a standard "slice of the action" approach: **she is more than £65,000 better off at the end**, because the overall tax cost has been almost halved using the alternative company route. However, there are several important hurdles to this simple model:

- Will Yasmin's sole property be considered a business eligible for Incorporation Relief? (Readers may be aware, however, that the watershed case EM Ramsay v HMRC [2013] UKUT 0226 turned in the taxpayer's favour, based on similar circumstances).

- HMRC *could* try to argue that the incorporation is an artificial component of a pre-ordained series of transactions (see 9.2.1) and that Yasmin should be taxed as if she had undertaken the project personally – i.e., basically back to the original scenario. But the element of risk / uncertainty in undertaking the development phase to sale on the open market would militate against any argument that the steps were pre-ordained.

- We have conveniently overlooked any additional cost of running the company, and how the company (or Yasmin personally in the original example, for that matter) might have financed the additional development costs, by assuming the project will still cost £200,000 overall, whether run personally or in a company.

- SDLT would be chargeable on the incorporation of the property: since the single block originally contained 8 dwellings, Yasmin may treat the dwellings as commercial property, costing a mere £24,500 SDLT in total.

- We have conveniently ignored the extra costs of undertaking a formal liquidation of the company as would be required to ensure that the distribution might be considered capital (see 16.6 "How to Liquidate a Company" below).

- We have also stretched the company's development phase over **2 years**, (April 2024 to March 2026), so that Yasmin will have held the shares for 2 years when she comes to liquidate the company – the new minimum qualifying holding period for Entrepreneurs' Relief/Business Asset Disposal Relief. (See Chapter 10; this is not implausible, given that it could easily take YasminCo many months or more to sell all of the new apartments on completion of the construction phase) Yasmin's personal tax costs might also be a bit lower, if the original purely personal ownership route were also stretched over 2 tax years. The question could arise of how Yasmin might be able to afford to wait for 2 years to extract funds from the corporate route (although depending on how much Yasmin needed, this could actually be achieved quite efficiently through the company, given the options potentially available).

- Even if Yasmin's share disposal passes all of the relevant tests for Entrepreneurs' Relief/Business Asset Disposal Relief at the point of liquidation, there are new "anti-phoenixing" rules that may apply to retrospectively change the distributions on liquidation to a much less tax-efficient dividend distribution instead, in some circumstances (see 16.6.3 "Phoenix Arrangements" below)

Note that in this context a profit motive is basically required to trigger the "Transactions in Land" regime on the development. If a property investor develops a formerly investment property for onward sale, then it is likely to be considered a trading-type venture from the point that the decision is made to develop the property for that profit. But if a property investor simply improves a property for the benefit of the ongoing letting business, then this should **not** be caught.

For example, if Yasmin in the above Case Study had wanted to develop the large block into smaller apartments *to make them easier for her to carry on letting*, then it should **not** have fallen within the scope of the Transactions in Land regime so to be subject to Income Tax, etc., when eventually sold; she should be subject to CGT on their disposal, instead. The timing of the development in relation to marketing and onward sale will be a key indicator.

Finally, the Transactions in Land regime does **not** apply where an individual develops his or her main residence for onward sale, and "only or main residence" CGT relief is available.

12.9. How Limited is Your Limited Liability?

One of the advantages of a company over a sole trade or a partnership is said to be the fact that the shareholder's liability is "limited" – see section 2.3 of this guide.

This is true as far as it goes, but in the real world, this "limited liability" can be... of limited benefit.

A company needs cash. When it first starts its business life, it can raise that cash from only one or two sources:

- By issuing shares in exchange for cash
- By borrowing money

The cash that shareholders put into the company when they subscribe for shares is, of course, at risk if things go wrong – "limited liability" means that, at worst, they will lose this money.

When a company borrows money, usually it can either borrow it from:

- Its shareholders, or
- Commercial lenders – such as banks

Clearly, if the money is borrowed from the shareholders, they are also at risk for that money if things go wrong (and note that if their company is in difficulties, there are strict rules against repaying shareholders' loans in preference to the company's other debts).

If the company borrows from a commercial lender (say, a bank), particularly when it is a fairly new company, it is quite likely that the bank will require a "personal guarantee" from one or more of the shareholders/directors.

A "personal guarantee" (known as a "PG") is a promise from the individual concerned that if the company fails to repay the money it has borrowed, then the individual will step in and repay the loan himself.

Typically, a PG will be backed up by a "charge" on the individual's other property – typically his or her home. A "charge" means that if the individual fails to repay the loan after the company defaults, then the bank can take that home and sell it to get its money back.

In many cases, therefore, the limited liability offered by a company will not be as good a protection as it might at first appear:

Case Study - 24   Limited Liability

Andrew sets up a company to develop a property. The company needs £250,000 to buy the property and to renovate it and sell it. The money comes from:

- Andrew's subscription for shares - £10,000
- Loan from Andrew (his life savings) - £40,000
- Loan from High Street Bank (with a PG from Andrew) - £200,000

The company buys the land and begins to develop it, but unfortunately discovers that there are old mine workings undermining the entire property.

Building work cannot continue, and the land is sold off at a knock-down price (being virtually useless for anything). When the dust settles, the company's assets are £100,000 in cash.

Because the £100,000 is not enough to repay the bank, they call in Andrew's PG (which is secured on his house), and he has to sell this in order to pay the £100,000 owed to the bank after it has taken all the company's cash.

Andrew also loses the £40,000 he had lent to the company, and his £10,000' worth of shares are now worth nothing. Andrew does not feel that his limited liability as a shareholder has been much help to him!

In certain other circumstances, a director may become liable for the company's debts even though he has not lent it any money, nor given any PGs.

If a director allows a company to continue in business when he knows (**or should have known**) that the company will not be able to pay its debts, then he can be sued for "wrongful trading", and can be required to provide funds to help the company pay off its creditors.

With effect from July 2020, HMRC also introduced new rules to make directors and shareholders, etc., jointly and severally liable for a company's tax debts, (like for a partner in a partnership – see 2.2 above), where:

- Their company has undertaken tax avoidance activity or similar, or
- The individual has been similarly involved with **at least two other companies** within the past 5 years, that have been subject to insolvency proceedings, with outstanding tax liabilities of £10,000 or more.

This is a complex new regime that has the potential to put some individuals – such as those running several construction projects in separate companies – to quite significant personal financial risk. See also 16.6.3 below.

For these reasons, directors whose companies are getting into financial trouble should not ignore the problem. They should seek their accountant's advice immediately, in order to avoid the risk of becoming personally liable if the company goes under.

13. Close Companies

All of the companies featured in the case studies in this guide are "close" companies. In this chapter we will become more familiar with this terminology and understand what it means.

13.1. What is a Close Company?

A "close" company is basically a UK company that is controlled by:

- Five or fewer "participators", or
- Any number of "participators", if those "participators" are also directors

A "participator", broadly, means a shareholder although loan creditors may, in some circumstances, also be participators.

Case Study - 25   Examples of Close Companies

Example of "close" companies include:

- The shares in Company A are owned equally by three individuals. Company A is a close company, because it is controlled by five or fewer participators

- The shares in Company B are owned **equally** by nine individuals. Company B is a close company, because any five out of the nine could control it

- The shares in company C are divided equally amongst five married couples. Company C is a close company, because when looking at "control" you include shares held by "associates" and spouses are associates of each other.

- The shares in company D are owned by ten directors who each hold 10% of the company's shares. Even though it would generally require six of those directors to exercise control, the company is still close because they are all directors of the company as well.

This is only a very broad summary of the rules defining a close company, because the detailed rules are extremely complicated, being designed to prevent people artificially creating a company which should be a close company but is not.

For the purposes of this guide, assume that any property investment or property development company you set up is going to be a close company.

13.2. Special Rules for Close Companies

There are certain special rules for close companies, which cover:

- The meaning of a "distribution" from the close company

- The tax on loans from the close company to its participators

- The way corporation tax is calculated for certain types of close company

13.3. The Meaning of a "Distribution" From a Close Company

If a close company provides any "benefits or facilities of whatever nature" to a participator (or his associates) in a close company, then this is treated as if the company had paid him a dividend equivalent to the benefit.

This does not apply if the participator is also a director or employee of the company, where the benefit will be charged to Income Tax as part of his or her remuneration from the company. It is therefore quite unusual to come across this alternative dividend scenario:

> **Case Study - 26   Distribution to a Participator**
>
> Closeco Ltd is a close company, and Daniel is one of the shareholders. Daniel is not a director and does not work for the company, and is not related to any of the other shareholders. The company manufactures TV sets, and one Christmas, it gives each of its shareholders a brand new TV.
>
> Most of the shareholders are directors of the company and so they are taxed on the TVs as a benefit in kind from their employment, but Daniel is not, so he is treated as if he had received a **dividend** equivalent to the cost to the company of the TV.
>
> If the cost of the TV is £1,000, then Daniel (a higher rate taxpayer) will be charged to income tax of £337.50.
>
> The company is able to claim a deduction for the cost of the TVs supplied to the directors (as a cost of employing them), but it cannot get a deduction for the cost of Daniel's TV – dividends are paid out of the company's **post**-tax profits (4.5.2).

13.4. Loan To Participator – "s455 Tax"

Much more common is a **loan to a participator**.

This will occur if the company lends money to one of its shareholders. The company will be required to pay tax under section 455 CTA 2010 on the amount of the loan (hence the nickname "section 455 tax").

For loans made on or after 6 April 2022, the rate of tax is 33.75% of the amount of the loan (for loans made between 6 April 2016 and 5 April 2022, it was 32.5%, and for many years before that date, the rate was 25%).

When the loan is repaid, HMRC will refund the tax. The timing is important.

Case Study - 27   Section 455 Tax

A close company makes a loan of £10,000 to a shareholder. When it puts in its Corporation Tax payment (nine months after its year-end), it must include section 455 tax of £3,375 in its tax payment – unless the loan is repaid within nine months of the end of that accounting period, in which case no section 455 tax is due. (If, for example, 60% of the loan is repaid in time, then only 40% of the original section 455 tax will actually be payable).

Assuming the loan is **not** repaid within nine months of the end of the accounting period in which it was made, then the section 455 tax will be due in full and will only be repaid nine months after the end of the accounting period in which the loan is actually repaid. (The same approach applies to part-repayments made after the initial nine-month deadline).

For example:
The company prepares its accounts for the calendar year, and on 31 December 2024 it lends £10,000 to a shareholder. The loan is repaid on 1 January 2026 – just over 12 months later (but, importantly, just into the *second* accounting period after the loan was actually made – the loan was outstanding for all of the accounting period ended 31 December 2025).

On 1 October 2025, the company pays its Corporation Tax in respect of the 2024 accounts year, and section 455 tax of £3,375.

On 1 October 2026, the company pays its Corporation Tax for the 2025 return year. It cannot yet claim back any section 455 tax, because although the loan has been repaid by now, it was repaid (just) after the end of the 2025 return year.

On 1 October 2027, the company pays its Corporation Tax due for the 2026 year, and, because it is now nine months after the end of the accounting period in which the loan was repaid, it can claim repayment of the section 455 tax.

Although the loan was only outstanding for one year and two days at the most, the section 455 tax is not repaid until two years after it had to be paid.

Some companies try to get around this by "bed and breakfasting" the loan:

The company makes up its accounts to the calendar year. On 1 January 2025, it lends £40,000 to a shareholder.

On 30 December 2025, the shareholder borrows £40,000 from her rich uncle, and repays the loan. She therefore owes nothing to the company at the end of the accounting year, 31 December 2025.

On 2 January 2026, she again borrows £40,000 from the company, and repays her uncle.

> On 30 December 2026, she borrows £40,000 from uncle... and so on!
>
> Because the loan never appears in the company's balance sheet at 31 December, the company believes there is no section 455 tax to pay – after all, the loan has been repaid, hasn't it?
>
> HMRC take the view that a temporary repayment of a loan in this way is not effective – it is very unwise for a company to rely on "bed and breakfasting" a loan in this way.
>
> **Legislation in CTA 2010 s 464 (as amended by FA 2013) specifically targets this practice of "bed and breakfasting" loans.** Depending on the size of the loan, the repayment is ignored (so the section 455 tax remains due) if it takes place less than 30 days before a further loan is made (loans over £5,000), or if there are "arrangements" in place for a further loan, at the time of the repayment (loans over £15,000).
>
> HMRC should, however, allow loan repayments to stand where those amounts have been paid out of salary or dividend that have been credited to the participator's loan account, rather than being paid out to him directly. Essentially, this is because HMRC is less concerned about "bed and breakfasting" of loan balances where the loans have been paid off using income from that company, that has been taxed on the participator already (or soon will be).

In order to get the section 455 tax repaid, the company can also write off the loan. In other words, the company formally declares that it will cancel the loan. The tax consequences of this are:

- The company can claim repayment of the section 455 tax as if the loan had been repaid (or if the loan is written off within 9 months of the accounting period in which it was made, no section 455 tax will be payable in the first place).

- The shareholder is taxed as if he or she had received a dividend equal to the loan being written off.

This can be used as a planning tool:

> **Case Study - 28   Write off or Cancellation of a Loan**
>
> In Case Study 10, we saw the problems that can arise if a company pays dividends to its shareholders that are not proportionate to their shareholdings. If instead of paying a dividend to the shareholders, the company lent them money and then wrote off the loan, they would get broadly the same tax effect as a dividend.
>
> The timing of the tax payment can be better, as well. Compare the timing of the tax payment between a dividend and a loan written off:
>
> The company makes up its accounts to the calendar year. Its Corporation Tax will therefore fall due for payment on 1 October, in the year following.

> In scenario A, it *pays a dividend* of £5,000 on 6 April 2024 to a shareholder, who pays Income Tax at the higher rate and has already used his new Dividend Allowance from other sources.
>
> In scenario B, it *lends* £5,000 to the same shareholder, also on 6 April 2024. It then formally cancels the loan on 6 April 2025 (i.e., less than 9 months after its year-end of 31 December 2024).
>
> In scenario A, the shareholder has received a dividend in the tax year 2024/25 He will be personally liable to pay Income Tax of £1,687 by 31 January 2026.
>
> In scenario B, the shareholder is deemed to have received a distribution (dividend) in the tax year 2025/26 (the tax year in which the loan was written off, **not** the tax year in which the loan was originally made). He will be liable to pay the same amount of Income Tax (£1,687), but not until 31 January 2027.
>
> Because the loan was formally written off within 9 months of the end of the accounting year in which it was made, the company does **not** have to pay any section 455 tax. In both scenarios, the shareholder has had the use of the money from 6 April 2024, but the date on which he has to pay income tax on it has been deferred by a year, in scenario B.

Caution

This particular planning technique is not as simple as it appears, and you should take advice from a Tax Adviser before using it. There are a number of aspects of company law to consider, and also the "preordained series of transactions" rules we have already looked at – see Case Study 15 and 9.2.1. There may also be issues with NIC and taxable benefits in kind to deal with, if the shareholder is also a director.

13.5. Beware Close Investment Holding Companies & "Properties Let Commercially"

The re-introduction of different Corporation Tax rates – the Small Companies Rate – as noted in Chapter 4 also revived the regime for "Close Investment-Holding Companies", or "CIHCs".

A CIHC is essentially a close company whose main role is to hold investments, and it arguably doesn't "do" anything active, such as carry on a trade.

Broadly, the government does not want to give the 19% starting rate for Small Companies to those companies that are not actively working to generate wealth, so **a CIHC is always taxable at the 25% Main Rate of Corporation Tax, no matter how low the profits.**

One key point to keep in mind with CIHCs is that **any company is a CIHC by default, except when it is not**. In other words, for each chargeable tax period, the company

has to meet criteria in order to escape the CIHC designation. Fortunately, the criteria are widely drawn, and include at the new CTA 2010 s 18N, broadly:
a) Where a company exists primarily for the purposes of carrying on a trade, (or trades), on a commercial basis
b) Where a company exists primarily for the purposes of making investments in land (including physical buildings) where the land is, or is meant to be, let commercially

This – (b) – is why most property businesses will NOT be CIHCs, and WILL carry on being able to claim the 19% Small Companies rate for (up to) the first £50,000 of taxable profits in a year.

This is worth emphasising because I have already encountered a number of advisers who believe that family companies undertaking rental investment businesses must be CIHCs because they are "close", and because they exist for the purpose of making investments – property letting. Fortunately, this is not the case.

But it is not quite so simple as that, because there is a nasty sting in the tail lurking for any company set up to let out property to a person who is connected with the company, or who is a close relative of a person connected with the company (note "person" can include companies as well as individuals – so one company may be connected with another company – but only individuals can have relatives!) See below for more on "connected" persons, etc.

When it comes to (a) above, and "carrying on a trade *on a commercial basis*" the phrase 'commercial basis' means what most people would expect it to mean, albeit refined by case law, etc. But when it comes to (b) and property letting, "let commercially" *actually* means 'let out to anyone who is **not** connected with the company'. **So, any company letting out property to either a shareholder, or to a close relative of a shareholder, WILL be more exposed to the CIHC regime.** Again, there are numerous exclusions, but they can become quite detailed, so it is better to take advice where this may be relevant.

Close Investment-Holding Companies: Further Points

Family Investment Companies – which may hold a wide range of investments – may well be exposed to CIHC status, unless for example their main activity is letting property on a commercial basis.

Note the especially punitive treatment for connected persons has parallels with the rules for the **Annual Tax on Enveloped Dwellings** – see 12.5

The definition of **"connected persons"** can become quite involved in the detail but we broadly mean where one party has the power to control another, or controls two other parties, usually by means of shares or voting rights. We typically assume that relatives and other 'associates' will themselves be connected, and pool their voting rights to exert control. However, the strict definition of "connection" (and "relatives") can vary according to where you are in the legislation – it varies through the tax code. My best recommendation in this regard would be, if you feel that two parties may be "connected" and that it may be relevant for tax purposes, ask your adviser to check for you.

14. The Directors' Tax Liabilities

So far, we have looked only at the tax that directors of a company will pay on salaries, dividends and loan write-offs (releases).

This chapter considers the other tax liabilities they may have in relation to the company.

14.1. Tax on Non-Cash Benefits

Directors (and other employees) are liable to tax on non-cash benefits they receive from the company that employs them. We shall refer only to "directors" in this book for simplicity.

The whole area of employee benefits is a complex and specialised branch of tax, but this chapter attempts to give some guidelines on the pitfalls to avoid, and one or two opportunities as well.

Directors are also potentially liable to tax on any business expenses that the company reimburses to them, (but not if they were incurred for business purposes, generally speaking – i.e., the potential taxable benefit of a reimbursement is cancelled out if the director can claim a business purpose for his or her expense that is being reimbursed).

14.2. Expenses

Directors may incur expenses when on the company's business. The most common example is travelling expenses.

14.2.1. Travelling expenses

The cost of business travel is an allowable expense, subject to certain exclusions. The one that most commonly causes problems is travel from home to work.

Travel from your home to your normal place of work is "ordinary commuting" and the cost is NOT allowable as a business expense. This can be a particular problem for the typical small family company.

If the company has a headquarters, such as a rented office in a town, or a yard where it keeps its building equipment, then travel from home to that place is unlikely to be an allowable expense.

If, on the other hand, the company's base of operations is the home of the controlling director, travel from his home to anywhere that the company's business is being conducted – such as a building site, or a property being refurbished – is usually an allowable expense.

If a property investment company uses a letting agent to administer the properties it lets, then it is likely that HMRC will argue that the business is being administered through the agent, and that therefore the director's home is just a home, and not where the company's business is carried on, even if the director brings paperwork home occasionally.

Any company whose directors are incurring significant travelling expenses should check with a Tax Adviser to confirm that the expenses are allowable – getting it wrong can be expensive, as we shall see in chapter 15, which deals with tax investigations.

14.2.2. Cars

Most travelling expenses involve the cost of running a car.

It used to be a good tax planning idea to have the company own a car, and to allow the director to use it for both business and private purposes, as the rules for taxing directors on their private use of a "company car" *used to be* quite generous.

These rules have been made progressively more punitive over the years, and it is now very unlikely that it will be beneficial for a director who also owns the company to have a company car that is available for private use.

There is no substitute for doing the calculations specific to the individual director and the particular car, but it nearly always turns out that he or she will be better off owning the car privately and charging the company for any business mileage, as below.

14.2.3. Using Your Own Car for Business

A director who uses his or her own car for business mileage can be reimbursed tax free by the company at a rate of 45p per business mile for the first 10,000 business miles in the tax year (year to 5 April), and at 25p per mile for any further business mileage.

Note that this is now the only reimbursement that is allowable for employee tax purposes. If the director instead claims the actual cost of his business mileage from the company – by keeping records of all running costs and of his business and private mileage – then, when the company pays him for these expenses, rather than a mileage rate, the payment is taxable. Where amounts paid by the company are less than the HMRC-approved rates, then the difference can be reclaimed on the director's tax return – provided they maintain adequate records of the business mileage incurred.

14.2.4. Using Cars for Sole Traders and Partnerships

A sole trader or partner in a property business **can** keep full records and claim the actual cost of the business miles, **or** he or she can opt for the flat rate mileage allowances described above. It is only employees (including directors) who cannot claim for their actual allowable costs any more, and must claim according to a mileage rate, with prescribed maximum rates.

14.2.5. Three Important Differences to Remember

This is an excellent example of three important differences between the tax treatment of companies and their directors, when compared to sole traders/partners:

- The relationship between a company and its director is more formal than that between a sole trader/partner and his or her business

- The rules for directors tend to be more restrictive and punitive, when compared to sole traders

- The differences between the two sets of rules defy common sense!

14.3. Other Expenses

Motoring expenses, providing the rules described above are followed, are not taxable on directors, but many other expenses *potentially* can be – for example:

- The company pays the director's train fare to visit a development site where the company is building some buy-to-sell properties.

- The director has to attend a meeting to close a deal on a new property, and because it is a long journey from his home, the company reimburses him for the cost of an overnight stay in a hotel.

- The directrix uses her own credit card to pay for goods or services for the company, and claims the cost back from the company.

- The directrix takes herself and her spouse on a night out to celebrate finishing a challenging development project, spending £500 in total.

> Following the abolition of "dispensations" in 2016, it is down to the employer to determine if an expense has been incurred for business purposes and may be considered non-taxable. Otherwise, it must be reported and will probably be taxable, unless the employee can claim otherwise. Of the four examples above, the first three will likely pass muster, and it is clearly the last that is problematic. There are in fact reasonably generous provisions relating to annual staff events and 'trivial' benefits in kind but the cost in this case would exceed those thresholds, and would need to be reported to HMRC.

Where taxable, they must either be reported on the company's annual return of benefits provided to a director/employee (traditionally known as a Form P11D) or, in the case of cash payments, they should strictly be paid under deduction of PAYE. Employers have the option to "payroll" some benefits rather than use the P11D reporting system.

HMRC announced at the beginning of 2024 that the old-fashioned annual P11D return was to be abolished with payrolling of benefits in kind being the only option from April 2026. For taxable benefits that remain relatively static through the year, then this will be relatively straight forward. But more complex benefits such as the provision of living accommodation or directors' loans, the payrolling process has yet to be resolved.

14.4. Shares as Rewards

We have seen how the company is owned by its shareholders, and how their shares entitle them to their proportion of dividends paid and, ultimately, to a share of the company's assets when it is wound up. For many years, shares have also been used as a way of providing rewards to employees, and in some cases as a means of trying to pay them in a way that escaped tax and NIC, or reduced their impact.

As a result, HMRC and the Treasury have introduced increasingly complex and punitive rules taxing employees and directors on the benefit of any "employment related securities" (encompassing shares, debentures and other securities) which they are given.

This is not the place for a detailed examination of these rules (that would take a book longer than this one) but the following Case Study illustrates the type of pitfall to watch out for.

> **Case Study - 29   Shares as Rewards**
>
> Mr Fox and Mr Hound each own very similar property development companies. They are both the sole shareholders, and they are both getting on in years.
>
> Mr Fox has two sons, who both work in the business, and he decides he would like to give them 24% of his shares each – Mr Fox is a great family man, and says he believes in "keeping the family business within the family". He will still have 52% of the shares, but if all goes well over the next few years, he will be able to hand over full control and enjoy a well-earned retirement.
>
> Mr Hound is in broadly the same situation and has exactly the same plans, except that in his case he has only one daughter, and no sons. He does, however, have a very loyal manager (not related to him and, though on good terms with the family, not a close friend), who has worked for the company for many years, and who could be trusted to help his daughter in running the company – "she has a good eye for property, and he is an excellent project manager", he explains. Mr Hound does exactly the same as Mr Fox – he gives 24% of his shares each to his daughter and the manager, with a view to handing over to them entirely in a few years if all goes well.
>
> Because Foxco Ltd and Houndco Ltd are both trading companies, Mr Fox and Mr Hound can "hold over" the capital gains tax on their disposals of their shares – which is just as well, because the shares are now worth tens of thousands of pounds – both companies are doing well and have a number of profitable projects on the go.
>
> The tax treatment of the recipients of the shares is very different, though.
>
> In the Fox brothers' case, HMRC will probably accept that the gift of the shares is covered by the **only** exception to the rules for "employment related securities", which excludes shares given to employees "in the normal course of the domestic, family, or personal relationships" of the person giving them.
>
> There are no income tax implications for the Fox boys.

> Miss Hound and the manager, however, are in a very different position. Because Miss Hound received her shares at the same time as the (unrelated) manager, it may be difficult to argue that hers were "domestic, family, or personal relationships" shares.
>
> It would certainly seem quite challenging to try to argue that the manager's shares were *not* in some way related to his job.
>
> You will also notice that Mr Fox was careful to stress the importance of family, and to downplay the obvious fact that he hoped the boys would be motivated to put more effort into the company once they owned a large slice of it, whereas Mr Hound could not resist mentioning what a good job the manager <u>and his daughter</u> were doing.
>
> As a result, Miss Hound and the manager are exposed to Income Tax on basically the market value of the shares they have been given and, in the particular circumstances of this case, there may even be a PAYE and NIC liability, which Houndco will have to pay, and then *further* tax liabilities if Miss Hound and the manager do not reimburse the company for that tax and NIC.
>
> If you think the distinction between the way the two companies were treated is exaggerated, please note that both Foxco and Houndco are based on real cases.

It is <u>never</u> safe to assume that if an employee or director (or their close family) acquires shares in the company he works for, then there will be no tax implications.

Even if **you** acquire your shares following the setting up of your own new company, it is possible that the company will be required to report the fact (on a "Form 42" or – now – its online equivalent, by 7 July after the end of the tax year in which you acquired the shares).

There are some narrow exceptions to this rule, but they are *very* narrow exceptions.

Always ask your Tax Adviser **before** you enter into **any** transaction involving shares and employees (including directors) – this is a complicated and 'dangerous' area, but to look on the bright side, there is much that can be done to reduce the tax burdens involved.

14.5. FIVE Tax Free Benefits

To end this Part on a more cheerful note, let us look at a few benefits that a company can provide to its directors without any tax liability arising.

Pensions
While advice on pensions is strictly the domain of a qualified independent financial adviser, where that qualified adviser *does* recommend a pension, then a company can provide an appropriate vehicle. Property investors in business on their own account, such as landlords, are usually quite limited in the qualifying pension contributions that they can make. This is because large pension contributions can only secure tax relief

if they are deemed to have been paid out of "relevant earnings", but rental income is generally treated as income from investments, not earnings.

While broadly any individual can pay up to £3,600 (gross) per year towards a pension even without any relevant earnings, an individual can get tax relief on larger contributions only if they have sufficient relevant earnings in that year. A limited company can either pay a salary from which an individual can make a personal contribution or, more likely, the company will make a contribution directly on the employee's behalf. HMRC will generally accept even very large lump sums paid to a pension scheme for a controlling shareholder/director as allowable, but caution is recommended if the proposal is to make large pension payments for a family member with only a modest role in the business – see HMRC's Business Income Manual at BIM46035 for more information on HMRC's approach.

The following tax free benefits provided below may seem trivial, but their value mounts up.

Car Parking
The company can provide any employee with a car parking space at or near his or her place of work (either in the company's own car park, or in a commercial car park). Since April 2018, this also applies to providing a charging point (and electricity) for employees' use. As electricity prices and battery capacities continue to rise, this can actually end up being quite a valuable benefit.

Mobile Phones
The company can provide a mobile phone – though since April 2006, this has been restricted to one phone per employee. Do **not** fall into the trap of simply reimbursing the director for his or her own, **personal** mobile contract and assuming that is the same thing – the latter is taxable and potentially NIC'able as well.

Child Care

Companies may in some cases be able to provide workplace nurseries or creche at the place of work, without a taxable benefit in kind or NICs.

Alternatively, the company can pay for childcare (in a commercial nursery or with an approved child-minder) for employees' children, up to a maximum of £55 per week per employee, free of tax. **This "childcare voucher" scheme was closed to new entrants from October 2018, but employees already enrolled in a voucher scheme can continue to use it until their qualifying children reach the maximum age.**

Note that this benefit must be offered to all employees. Of course, this may not be an issue if the company has only one or two directors and no other employees.

The level of tax free childcare vouchers varies according to the amount of other income the individual concerned has from the company.

In theory, since 2011, this relief is restricted for higher earners, but the restrictions are potentially quite easy to circumvent for a family company.

Meals
On the basis they are available to all employees, free meals in a works canteen or in the business premises (e.g. sandwich lunches) are tax free, provided they are "on a

reasonable scale" (so no caviar sandwiches!). Note that the exemption does not apply to meals in cafes, restaurants, or pubs.

Case Study - 30   Tax Free Benefits

Mr and Mrs Laurel have a property company. They are the directors, and there are no other employees. The company provides them with the following benefits:

- A parking space each (they have two cars, and often one of them needs to go off alone, to visit a site for example) in the multi-storey near the company's office. The cost is £40 per week each

- A mobile phone each – cost £60 per month each

- Childcare for their two-year-old twins – cost £55 per week each

- Sandwich lunches eaten at their desks when they are in the office – cost £20 per week each

The total yearly cost of these benefits is £13,120 (based on 45 working weeks in the year in the case of the sandwiches). The company gets a tax deduction for all of these costs, so the actual cost is only £9,643 after taking account of the tax relief in the company of 26.5% (see 4.1).

Mr and Mrs Hardy have a similar company, and incur all the same expenses as those above, but they pay for them out of their (taxed) dividend income because they wrongly assume they would have to pay tax on these particular benefits in kind if the company provided them.

In order to have £13,120 to spend on these expenses, they need to draw sufficient dividends from the company, on which they pay tax at 33.75%, so the total extra dividend required is £19,803 (remember, the company does not get any tax relief for the cost of a dividend).

By using the company to pay expenses they would have incurred anyway, the Laurels have saved over £10,000. Director/shareholders should note, however, that these benefits should **not** be offered to any employee (directors included) alongside a cash alternative – **HMRC has significantly tightened up on so-called "salary sacrifice arrangements"** and, although childcare vouchers are protected, other benefits can be taxed as if the employee had taken the cash alternative instead!

15. Companies and Tax Investigations

HMRC have the power to "enquire" into any tax return from a company, a partnership, or an individual. They do not have to give a reason for the enquiry.

These "enquiries" come in several different forms, and this Part concentrates on the types of enquiry a company may face.

A sole trader or partnership is just as likely to face an enquiry, but as we shall see in this chapter, there are certain special features when a company is involved.

15.1. "Aspect" Enquiries

These are the least serious type of Enquiry – though they have been known to develop into "Full Enquiries" as they progress.

In an Aspect Enquiry, the inspector will ask questions about a specific issue in the company's tax return – a favourite example for a property letting/investment company would be to check if amounts claimed for repairs to a let property are in fact improvements to it (that cannot be deducted from annual rental profits, although they may instead be allowed for CGT, when the property is sold, for example). A common query for property development companies would be whether or not projects in progress at the accounts year-end had been correctly valued, so as to recognise an appropriate level of profit.

Many Aspect Enquiries are closed down with no penalties being charged – though this is not always the case if large or blatant errors are found – but there will be interest to pay on any additional tax that is collected, running from the date the tax would have been paid if the return had been correct in the first place.

15.2. "Compliance" Enquiries

This is a term for Enquiries aimed at checking that the business has complied with its obligations under the various laws and regulations it is obliged to obey. For property businesses, the commonest are:

- **Construction Industry Scheme (CIS) compliance**
  The CIS applies to all property developers (but not normally to property investors – see section 8.3 above), and requires them to check the credentials of all the subcontractors they use, and record all payments to them, while in some cases deducting tax from those payments.

  See our other guide "**Tax Tips for Property Developers and Renovators**" for more details of the CIS and the procedure for HMRC checks on compliance.

- **PAYE and benefits in kind**
  A sole trader or partnership will be liable to this type of Enquiry only if it has employees, but ANY company could face one – because its directors are employees for tax purposes.

  The Enquiry will check if the company has operated PAYE correctly, and if all benefits in kind and expenses payments have been correctly reported on the annual Forms P11D, or payrolled correctly.

- **VAT**
    HMRC will (for example) check that any property purchases have been handled correctly regarding Transfer of a Going Concern issues and that "options to tax" (charge VAT) have been exercised correctly on commercial buildings; for companies making both VAT'able and exempt supplies – common in companies dealing with both residential and commercial property – then VAT Partial Exemption calculations are likely to be scrutinised.

    Finally, the Capital Goods Scheme applies to properties (potentially including developments) costing more than £250,000 before VAT; very simply, when you buy such a property and VAT is in point, then you may have to monitor how it is used for up to 10 years, to make sure you haven't over claimed VAT. This often catches out businesses that sell or let out commercial property (on which they have – quite understandably – reclaimed VAT on initial purchase), but where they neglected to opt to tax their interest in the property beforehand.

- **Business Records Inspections**
    HMRC also have the power to visit business premises and inspect the books and the business assets. They can do this either by prior arrangement, or if they get authorisation from the Tax Tribunal, they can turn up unannounced. Note that you only have to let them in if they have authorisation from the Tribunal – if the authorisation is only signed by a senior HMRC officer you can tell them to go away and make an appointment. (Strictly, you do not have to let them in even if they *have* been authorised by the Tax Tribunal, but you may be charged up to £300 as a civil penalty unless you have a good reason for the refusal).

15.3. Full Enquiry

This is the type of Enquiry that is generally referred to as a Tax Investigation, and it will involve the inspector looking at all the business accounts and records, and in some cases the private bank statements, etc., of the owners or directors. It may also involve some or all of the more specialised types of Enquiry referred to above.

This is not the place for a detailed examination of how to deal with a tax investigation, but there is one vital piece of advice – **do not attempt to deal with it yourself!** In particular, if you or your company receive a notice from the tax inspector to say he has decided to "Enquire" into your or your company's return, **seek professional help immediately** – in the first instance, from your accountant, though in serious cases he or she may well want to call in tax specialists like us.

There are two specific problem areas in investigations that are peculiar to companies (though the first could also apply to a sole trader or partnership if they had employees):

15.4. "Grossing up"

Where an employee (including a director) has received payments that should have been made under PAYE, the inspector will generally argue that the tax liability should be settled by the employer rather than the employee, and that this should be done by "grossing up" the payments made.

Case Study - 31   Grossing Up

A company has paid a weekly cash sum of £50 to its directors to cover "general expenses". It is agreed that this "round sum payment" should have been paid under PAYE through the payroll.

The directors are higher rate taxpayers, so for each director to have received £50 in cash, the PAYE deductions would have been:

Gross payment	85
Less Income Tax at 40%	(34)
Less Employees' NIC at 2%	(1)
Gives weekly cash	50

In addition, the company would have had to pay employers' NIC at 13.8% on the £85 – another £11.

So, for each director involved, the annual amount of tax and NIC the inspector will seek to claim **for each year under enquiry** will be:

Weekly income tax	34
Weekly employee NIC	1
Weekly employer's NIC	11
Weekly total	46
Times 52 gives	2,438

(Note – the PAYE year is sometimes 53 weeks long, and also note it is HMRC practice to round down to the nearest pound)

"Grossing up" does not always happen – but it is almost always the position HMRC starts from, and you will need a Tax Adviser who has experience of negotiating with HMRC on these cases to ensure the damage is limited as much as possible.

15.5. Company Investigation Settlements

Company Investigation Settlements are also complicated by the way that companies and their directors are regarded by HMRC when it is found that tax has been lost, particularly as a result of undeclared income.

Case Study - 32   Undeclared Income in a Company

Mr Burke is a sole trader, and when his return and accounts are investigated, it is found that he has failed to include £10,000 income for the year – the rent from a property he owns.

The inspector explains that Mr Burke should have paid £4,000 Income Tax on this income, and so Mr Burke will have to pay:

Tax	4,000
Interest for late payment (say)	200
Penalties at 35% of tax (see later in this Part)	1,400
Total	5,600

(in reality, it is also quite possible that the £10,000 omitted income would be "scaled back" through the previous six years, perhaps using the Retail Price Index to estimate how much was missing in those years – see 15.6 below)

Mr Burke agrees to this, pays up, and that is the end of the matter. Now let's look at a similar situation but this time in a company

Mr Hare is the sole shareholder and director of a company, and it is found that £10,000 rental income has gone missing from his company's accounts and found its way into his pocket.

The tax consequences are more complicated, because HMRC takes the view that sums "misappropriated" by director/shareholders are in effect loans to them from the company – "loans to participators" (see 13.4 above).

This means that:

- The company has "lent" Mr Hare £10,000, and HMRC will insist that he pays it back as a condition of settling the Enquiry. If Mr Hare does not have the money, then the company may have to pay him a dividend to fund the repayment – Income Tax for Mr Hare of £3,375 (assuming he is a Higher Rate taxpayer and his Dividend Allowance has already been used)

- The company owes section 455 tax (see Case Studies 25 to 27) of £3,375. Although this will be repaid when Mr Hare repays the "loan", the company

> will still have to pay interest on it from the date the company should have paid the section 455 tax.
>
> - By lending the money interest-free to Mr Hare, the company has given him a benefit in kind, and he will have to pay Income Tax based on the official rate of interest (2.25% currently), so Mr Hare is taxed on a benefit equating to £225 per year) – but this normally only runs from the date he agrees that the cash has been misappropriated until the day he repays it.
>
> - The company should have paid corporation tax at 19% on the £10,000 of missing profit, so it owes at least £1,900 (depending on whether or not the addition means total taxable profits exceed £50,000 from April 2023, in which case the rate will be higher – see 4.1).
>
> - As with Mr Burke, there will be interest and penalties on all this.
>
> I have not offered a total of Mr Hare's and his company's costs, because these are so much a matter for negotiation with HMRC that any figure given could be misleading.
>
> Note also that the "scaling back" to earlier years referred to with Mr Burke could apply here as well, so the amount Mr Hare will have to repay to the company could be very large indeed.

I have mentioned penalties, and it is important to understand how these are calculated, because it is possible to reduce them if the investigation is properly handled.

Penalty calculations start from the amount of the tax that has been wrongly underpaid – 100% of this is generally the maximum possible penalty, although things can be worse if there is an offshore aspect.

The actual penalty depends on:
- whether the taxpayer disclosed the error before HMRC enquired into his affairs
- whether the omission was "careless", "deliberate" or "deliberate and concealed"
- how helpful the taxpayer is in quantifying the tax lost

The rates of penalty for these various levels of misbehaviour are:

	Prompted disclosure	Mistake despite reasonable care	Failure to take reasonable care – "careless"	Deliberate understatement	Deliberate understatement with concealment
1.	Max	0%	30%	70%	100%
2.	Min:	0%	15%	35%	50%
3.	Max reduction for prompted (1. – 2.)	0%	15%	35%	50%

	Unprompted disclosure	Mistake despite reasonable care	Failure to take reasonable care – "careless"	Deliberate understatement	Deliberate understatement with concealment
4.	Max	0%	30%	70%	100%
5.	Min:	0%	0%	20%	30%

| 6. | Max reduction for prompted (4. – 5.) | 0% | 30% | 50% | 70% |

> **Case Study - 33   Penalty Calculation**
>
> Mr Burke had failed to declare £10,000 income (by not declaring rent he received from a property). The level of his penalties was agreed as 35%, on the basis that this was a "deliberate understatement", but he did not then attempt to conceal it and he cooperated in reaching a settlement

15.6. Be Careful what the Inspector "Presumes"

When HMRC opens an enquiry, it *should* send out some quite lengthy standard paperwork that sets out what the taxpayer should expect, discussing co-operation, penalties, and such like. An enquiry may take several months to resolve, even if the Inspector is eventually satisfied that there is (little or) nothing that requires adjustment. By this time, the taxpayer will have become quite focused on specific transactions or treatments. We have already warned that penalties can be a painful addendum. But you should keep one or two specific issues in mind, rather than getting ambushed by the summary calculation just at the point you thought everything had been agreed (these apply to all enquiries, not just companies):

Continuity – If the Inspector finds that the taxpayer has done something like fail to declare all of their rental income, the Inspector will be keen to assume that the taxpayer has likewise failed to declare all of their rental income in the previous several tax years – this can easily be up to 4 years prior, but will be up to 6 years prior where the Inspector believes that the taxpayer was careless (or 20 years, where the offending behaviour was deliberate). This is referred to as a "presumption of continuity".

Hence what the taxpayer may have been lulled into thinking was an argument over £10,000 of income that may or may not have been declared, is very often really an argument over whether or not somewhere between £40,000 and £60,000 of income may have been omitted. (Strictly, the Inspector should adjust previous years' income figures for inflation, or similar, but the key point is that there may well be several years standing behind the original enquiry year, and this is easily forgotten over the course of a long enquiry). **It is very important that the "presumption of continuity" be challenged, where appropriate**.

Careless behaviour – HMRC likes to be offended by the very idea that it will *presume* taxpayers have been careless by default, preferring instead that it *may* find that a taxpayer has been careless in the course of the enquiry. I will say only that I am continually offended by how quickly and frequently an enquiry officer assumes that the taxpayer has been careless. **Again, whether or not the taxpayer has been careless is often a key factor in the scale of the penalty (if any) and the overall assessment, and it should be challenged, where appropriate.**

For any reader who doubts just how "careless" HM Inspector can be in their own deliberations, I might suggest the following tax cases:

- Angel Eyes Beauty Parlour Ltd v HMRC [2019] UKFTT 0247 (TC)
- Georgiou et al v HMRC [2022] UKFTT 00455 (TC)

- Café Jinnah LLP v HMRC [2024] UKFTT 159 (TC)

15.7. Watch Out for the Contractual Disclosure Facility (CDF) and COP 9

There is one further kind of investigation to consider. This is where HMRC believe there has been serious tax fraud. In these cases, they will send you a **Contractual Disclosure Form** under **Code of Practice 9 ("COP 9").**

If you are ever sent a CDF, it is **ABSOLUTELY ESSENTIAL** to take expert advice **immediately**. **UNDER NO CIRCUMSTANCES** try to handle this yourself, and, at the risk of offending the profession, it is unlikely that your regular accountant will have the expertise to deal with a CDF investigation.

15.8. Four Golden Rules of Tax Investigations

To end this part, here are the golden rules for dealing with tax enquiries:

- DON'T try to handle it yourself – get advice before you reply to the initial letter from the inspector, and at all costs DON'T ring the inspector up to "have a chat and sort this out"

- DON'T ignore it and hope it will go away – remember the mitigation of penalties for co-operation

- DO be honest and upfront with your Tax Adviser – only then will he or she be able to help you

- DO talk to your accountant about taking out insurance to cover the fees for a tax investigation – the professional fees can be very expensive

16. Getting Your Exit Strategy Right

It seems appropriate to include this towards the end of this guide, but in fact, **you should be thinking about your proposed exit route from the first day you start your business,** as it may affect how you set it up and the strategic decisions you make as time goes on.

16.1. Everybody Has an Exit Strategy

Some businessmen say they have no exit route – they will work 'til they drop, and leave the business to their children – but that is itself an exit route, and one we shall consider further in chapter 17.

16.2. The THREE Most Common Exit Strategies

If you decide not to leave the business to your children then it is highly likely you will adopt one of the following three possible exit routes:

- Sell the business as a going concern
- Liquidate the business and invest the cash in something else
- Keep the business as a source of retirement income

16.3. Selling the Business

For the sole trader or partner, there is little distinction between selling the business as a going concern, and simply selling off the business assets. In either case, he or she will pay CGT on the gain made from the sale of the business assets, and the main issue will be whether or not Entrepreneurs' Relief (Business Asset Disposal Relief) is available (see Chapter 10).

For a company, there will be a choice to make between:

- Selling the shares in the company
- The company sells its assets and the cash balance is then extracted from the company

It often happens that the decision is made for the company, because the purchaser insists either on buying the shares, or on buying the assets.

A purchaser will probably be thinking along these lines:

16.3.1.   Benefits of Buying the Shares in the Company

- Simplicity – the company is already up and running and all the buyer has to do is take it over. If the business name is important, buying the company is the simplest way to acquire the name (though this can be managed in other ways if assets are purchased).

- Stamp Duty – there is a flat rate of 0.5% for purchases of shares, whereas the Stamp Duty Land Tax on the purchase of land and property can be as high as 5% - or 15%, in the case of residential property (ignoring acquisitions by foreign investors).

- Financing – particularly if the purchaser is a listed company, it can offer its own shares in exchange for the shares in the business – more on this later.

16.3.2. Drawbacks of Buying the Shares in the Company

- History - when you buy a company's shares, you buy its history, including any skeletons it may have in its closet – for example, if the company has been getting its PAYE wrong, the problem will become yours once you own the shares, including any liabilities for years before you bought it.

    It is for this reason that Sale Agreements for companies tend to be more complicated than those for business assets alone, because they will (or should!) contain complex "warranties" (essentially, promises by the vendor that the company has no skeletons in the closet) and "indemnities" (promises by the vendor to pay for the funerals of any skeletons that do turn up after all).

- Tax – in some circumstances, the purchaser may be able to get more tax reliefs for his purchase if he buys assets rather than the company – to take only one example, if a company buys business assets (not shares in a company) that include certain intangible assets, the company may be able to get a tax deduction for the cost.

- Structure – if the purchaser already has a company, she may not want to buy another; if she does *not* already have a company, she may not want to run the business as a company.

From the vendor's point of view, there is a different set of considerations:

16.3.3. Benefits of Selling the Shares in the Company

- "Clean break" – by selling the company, he or she gets rid of its history – though this is subject to the warranties and indemnities that will probably be required.

- CGT – especially if the shares qualify for Entrepreneurs' Relief/Business Asset Disposal Relief, it is likely that he or she will pay less tax than if the company sells the assets (the company cannot itself claim ER/BADR).

- Avoiding double taxation – assuming the vendor wants the cash for himself, there is a "double whammy" if the company sells its business and is then liquidated, because the company will pay tax on the capital gains it makes on the sale of the assets, and then there will be another tax cost in the owner then extracting the funds from the company.

16.3.4. *Benefits of Selling the Company's Assets and then Liquidating*

I am tempted to say, "none", but it is always worth working the numbers for each individual case just to make sure.

The most common reason for asset sales is that the purchaser insists on it.

16.4. Selling the Company's Shares

The basic proposition is quite simple – the shareholder(s) of the company sell their shares, and they make a capital gain based on the difference between the price they sell for, and the cost of those shares when they subscribed for them (typically very low – maybe even £1), or otherwise acquired them.

If the company is a trading company, they may get ER/BADR (see Chapter 10), and the effective rate of tax they pay on the sale may be as low as 10%; otherwise (such as with a property investment company), they will pay CGT at 20%.

The reality, of course, is much more complicated, and it is essential to bring in a Tax Adviser at an early stage in all but the very simplest of company sales.

It is impossible to set out the "correct" strategy for selling a company.

Each company sale will have its own unique features, opportunities, and problems.

What follows are some examples of the kinds of situations that commonly arise:

16.4.1. *"Earn-outs"*

These are a very common feature of company sales. Essentially, the shares are sold for a cash sum up front, and with the promise of more cash depending on the company's performance over, say, the next three years. Points to consider with "earn-outs" include:

- Taxation of the earn-out. This can be complicated. If the deferred payments are **fixed**, such as "£100,000 on 31 March 2024, and £100,000 on 31 March 2025", then for tax purposes the vendor will be treated as receiving the **whole sum on the day he sells the company**.

    There are provisions for the CGT to be paid by instalments, and for repayments of CGT if the earn-out is never actually paid.

    If the deferred payments are uncertain at the time the company is sold – such as "40% of the profits made by the company in the next two years" – the treatment is different.

    The right to these future payments has to be valued at the time of the sale, and this value is taxed as part of the sale proceeds.

When and if the earn-out payments are made, the vendor is taxed on the difference between the value originally ascribed to the earn-out, and the amount then received.

Case Study - 34   Taxation of Uncertain Earn-Out

Sam sells his trading company for £200,000 cash up front, and 40% of the profits of the company in the year after the sale, payable four months after the end of that year when the accounts are signed off.

For the last three years the company's profits have averaged £250,000, so if all goes well, Sam expects to receive £100,000 for the earn-out. The cost of Sam's shares was a nominal £1, as he started the company himself from scratch three years ago.

It is agreed with HMRC that at the time of the sale, the value of the right to 40% of next year's profits, payable in 16 months' time, is £60,000. (This valuation takes account of both the fact that the amount of the payment is uncertain, and that Sam will have to wait for his money). On the sale of the company, Sam's CGT computation looks like this:

Sale cash	200,000
Value of earn-out	60,000
Total gain	260,000
CGT (after ER/BADR)	26,000

16 months later, it turns out that the company's profits were £200,000 for the year, so Sam's earn-out payment is £80,000.

His tax computation looks like this:

Payment received	80,000
Less value of earn-out	(60,000)
Taxable gain	20,000

Note that Sam gets no Entrepreneurs' Relief (Business Asset Disposal Relief) on the **additional** £20,000 – at that stage, he is not disposing of a qualifying business asset, but a "legal right" to more money.

16.4.2. *"Employment-Related Shares or Securities"*

If the vendor is required to stay on as a director of the company for the earn-out period, as often happens so that he can "hand over the reins" to the new owners (and make sure his earn-out is as big as possible), great care needs to be taken to make sure that he does not fall foul of the rules on "employment related securities" – see case Study - 28.

If the earn-out is paid in the form of loan notes or shares there is a danger that these will be treated as chargeable to Income Tax (on their market value) rather than to CGT – again, there are potentially ways around this, with good tax advice on the specific circumstances

16.4.3. *Payments Under Warranties and Indemnities*

The vendor often has to agree to pay the purchaser some sort of compensation if the company turns out not to be worth as much as he was told, or if there are unexpected tax liabilities.

It is important that the Sale Agreement is so worded that these are treated as refunds of the purchase price so that the vendor can get a CGT repayment, and the purchaser is not taxed on the payment until he or she eventually sells the shares.

16.4.4. *"Compensation for Loss of Office"*

There is an exemption from Income Tax and NIC for up to £30,000 paid to an employee who is sacked or made redundant, and Sale Agreements for companies quite often include provisions for £30,000 to be paid to the vendor (if he or she is expected to resign as director when the shares are sold).

Most of these "compensation payments" do not actually fall within the exemption as intended, and can cause tax problems for both the vendor and the company (which will then go for compensation from the vendor under the warranties and indemnities).

In some circumstances, these payments can be made tax free, but again this is an area for expert advice.

16.4.5. *Pre-Sale Tax Planning*

This ranges from simple things like getting cash out of the company before the sale (as most vendors are not prepared to "buy" cash in a company's bank account), through more sophisticated ideas like the ones mentioned above concerning earn-outs, to positively heroic enterprises such as moving to a tax haven for five years to escape CGT entirely (and yes, it has to be for five complete years, and no, it does **not** always work as planned – particularly now that the sale of shares in foreign companies that derive most of their value from UK land and property may still be caught – see 12.6.1 above).

16.4.6. Company Purchase of Own Shares

In some cases, rather than sell the shares to the purchaser directly, it may be possible for the company itself to buy them back from the vendor.

Case Study - 35   Company Purchase of Own Shares

Bill and Ben (who are not related) own 50% each of the shares in a trading company. Bill is older than Ben, and wants to retire. Bill and Ben agree that Bill's shares are worth £200,000, but Ben cannot afford to buy him out.

The company has £100,000 cash, however, and can easily raise another £100,000 on the security of its factory, which is owned by the company.

Bill's Tax Adviser explains that provided certain conditions are fulfilled, and a "clearance" is obtained from HMRC, it will be possible for the company to buy Bill's shares from him, and for the sale to be treated as giving rise to a capital gain for Bill – (normally, if a company buys shares back from its shareholders, this is treated as if the company has paid them a dividend, which is likely to be much more expensive).

The "clearance" is obtained, and the company buys Bill's shares for £200,000. Bill pays CGT on his gain (at 10% because of Entrepreneurs' Relief/BADR).

The effect of the company buying these shares is that they cease to exist, and so **Ben is now the sole owner of the company**.

This special treatment is only available to a company that is *trading*. If the shares in a property *investment* company are bought back, this will be treated as if the company had paid a dividend to the retiring shareholder.

16.4.7. Timing

Capital Gains Tax on most assets is payable on 31 January after the end of the year of assessment in which the gain is made, so for a sale on 5 April 2025 (i.e., in 2024/25, the tax is due on 31 January 2026.

For a sale a day later on 6 April 2025 (i.e., in 2025/26), the tax is payable a whole year later, on 31 January 2027.

However, CGT on account of the personal disposal of residential properties by individuals who are resident in the UK is payable within 60 days of completion, broadly since 6 April 2020. This will effectively count as a prepayment of the CGT that would otherwise be due under Self-Assessment, thereby marginally improving the Treasury's cashflow, at significant inconvenience to everyone else. UK companies are not caught by this new measure. For disposals by parties not resident in the UK, see 12.6.1.

Bear in mind that for CGT, a disposal generally takes place on the date the contract is signed and becomes "unconditional", and not, if later, the day the asset is transferred to the new owner, so simply exchanging contracts on 5 April with completion at a later date will **not** typically push the sale into the next tax year.

"Options" can be used to try to "lock in" the deal, but delay it to the next tax year.

(An "option" is simply an agreement between A and B that, should the option be exercised, A will sell an asset to B at a future date – a "call" option, or that B will buy the asset from A – a "put" option).

16.4.8. Gifts to Spouse / Civil Partner

Gifts generally attract CGT, and tax law requires that – for CGT purposes – the proceeds are set at the asset's market value, not £nil. Many people lose sight of this important principle, having become perhaps too comfortable with the rule that broadly says that gifts between spouses and civil partners does **not** trigger a CGT charge.

In some circumstances, it may be sensible to make use of that special treatment and to make a gift of some of your shares to your spouse or civil partner before the onward sale, to use their annual exemption (£3,000 for 2024/25 = £600 tax saved at 20%, **plus** up to another £37,700 at 10% because basic rate taxpayers pay CGT at just 10%), depending on how much of their band is "spare", but there are pitfalls:

- **Entrepreneurs' Relief/Business Asset Disposal Relief.** You can sometimes lose ER/BADR on some of the gain if you gift some of your shares to your spouse – they may not be eligible. Check with your tax adviser before making the gift.

- **"Imperfect" gifts.** Make sure you actually do make the gift, and that you do it before the sale has been agreed, and that the spouse is then included in the Sale Agreement (it is surprising how often this last point is forgotten).

    HMRC are becoming particularly hot on this point – if the gift is not properly evidenced or if the onward sale has already been agreed when the gift is made, HMRC will argue that all that was given was an entitlement to a proportion of the sale proceeds, and not the shares themselves. The implication is that the sale was in fact made by the original shareholding spouse/civil partner.

16.4.9. Substantial Shareholding Exemption

This only applies when a company sells its shares in another company, not when an individual sells shares.

In certain circumstances, (there are numerous criteria), a company is exempt from tax on a capital gain it makes when it sells shares in another company that it owns.

The details of this relief are complex, but very broadly, if a trading company has owned more than 10% of the shares in another trading company for at least a year, and it then sells those shares, it may qualify for the exemption and not have to pay Corporation Tax on any gain it makes on those shares.

Of course, from the point of view of the shareholders in the vendor company, they still have to find a way to get the cash out of that company.

16.4.10. Post-Sale Tax Planning

There is much less scope for this than there is for pre-sale tax planning, which is why it is important to take tax advice **before** a sale.

16.4.11. Tax Shelters

This does not refer to "tax haven" countries, but to approved investments that offer tax deferral, such as the EIS – see section 11.2.1.

16.4.12. Losses

Losses on sales of assets in the same or an earlier tax year can be set against gains of a tax year so, if contemplating a disposal standing at a substantial gain, now might be the time to sell off assets that will produce a loss (but remember also that a loss must be *claimed*).

16.5. Sales of Assets and Liquidation of Company

Although it is seldom the most tax efficient way to dispose of a company, this route is often forced on the vendor because the purchaser refuses to buy the shares instead, perhaps for the reasons already explained earlier in this section.

Once the assets of the business have been sold by the company, and it has paid the resulting corporation tax on its gains, we are left with what is sometimes known as a "cash-box" company – that is, a company whose only asset is a large bank balance. Unless the company plans to use this cash to start a new business venture, of course, the next question is how to get the cash out.

What happens next?

If the company pays the cash out to its shareholders as a dividend, they will suffer income tax at 33.75% on that dividend (assuming they are higher rate taxpayers), or even at 39.35% to the extent that the dividend takes their taxable income over £125,140 (see 1.1).

The alternative is to wind up the company and distribute its assets to its members.

This will ideally be treated as a disposal of their shares for CGT purposes, and so they will pay CGT based on the cost of their shares. It is possible to secure a 10% effective tax rate on capital gains, thanks to Entrepreneurs' Relief / Business Asset Disposal Relief (see Chapter 10).

16.6. How to Liquidate a Company

There are two ways a company can be liquidated – the formal way, and the informal way.

16.6.1. A Formal Liquidation

A formal liquidation must be undertaken by a specialised accountant called a "licensed insolvency practitioner".

It tends to be expensive (not least because in some circumstances a licensed insolvency practitioner can become personally liable to the company's creditors if he or she gets things wrong!), but it is sometimes necessary due to the nature of the company's business – ask your accountant to advise you. Given that distributions are usually treated as capital rather than as income following the appointment of a liquidator, it may also be desirable if the company has assets of more than £25,000 – see below.

16.6.2. An Informal Liquidation

This form of liquidation is also known as **"striking-off"**. This used to be by far the commonest form of liquidation, and it goes like this:

- The company pays all its debts and collects everything owed to it.

- The company pays out all its cash to its shareholders (it is also possible for the company to transfer any remaining assets it may have such as a property, though this is a little more complicated to arrange). The shareholders are basically treated as if they had sold their shares for the amount of cash or other assets they receive.

- Finally, the company applies to the Registrar of Companies to be "struck off" the Register of Companies. Once the Registrar has done this the company is dead – though, like Dracula, it can sometimes be revived if unforeseen liabilities appear.

Since March 2012 it is recommended to use this "informal" method only if the company's total assets at the point of contemplating striking off are less than £25,000. If more than this is to be distributed following the business' cessation, the whole amount may need to be treated as an income dividend under the informal route, so a formal liquidation may be preferred, despite the additional cost, in order to try to secure CGT treatment.

16.6.3. But Beware "Phoenix Arrangements"

Many readers will have heard of "phoenixing", whereby a company's shareholders may liquidate a company, and then set up a quite similar company a short while later, to rise from the ashes of the first. There is actually tax legislation to preserve losses when this happens, so that the successor company can benefit from losses made by the 'old' company (but there are rules within that legislation which seek to ensure that those losses may be transferred only if the successor company takes on at least some of the debt burden of its predecessor).

Unsurprisingly, however, HMRC takes a rather dim view of phoenix arrangements where the old company had significant PAYE, VAT or other unfulfilled tax liabilities when it died. HMRC has powers to:

- Require security deposits from businesses in relation to VAT, PAYE and NICs, where it perceives a risk that it may fail to settle its liabilities in future; from 6 April 2019, these powers were extended to allow HMRC to require security deposits also for Corporation Tax and for Construction Industry Scheme deductions.

- In quite rare circumstances, to pursue PAYE and NICs debts from certain employees, (typically the company's directors), rather than from the employing company

- The Finance Act 2020 contained provisions to allow HMRC to make a company's directors and shareholders jointly and severally liable for a company's tax liabilities, very broadly where:
    - The company has entered into tax avoidance arrangements or engaged in tax evasive conduct, and the company is subject to (or at serious risk of) insolvency, or
    - There have been two or more cases where previous related companies have gone into insolvency within the last 5 years, where tax liabilities have been at least £10,000

Simply put, such measures have previously been considered only in circumstances where HMRC realises that a director/shareholder had already participated in a business which failed, leaving significant debts owing to HMRC, and HMRC sees a risk that the same will happen again (although this is not a necessary precursor to either course of action).

The Finance Act 2020 provisions, allowing HMRC to make directors and shareholders personally liable for their company's tax liabilities where repeated phoenixism appears to have occurred, are significantly wider in their scope, could easily capture innocent property developers who often work through multiple companies, and have been widely criticised – not least because they can even make directors and shareholders personally liable for old companies' tax liabilities that arose up to 5 years beforehand.

One consequence of the government's decision to tax capital gains rather less than income, is that it now perceives risk from moneybox companies and phoenix arrangements, where a company does not distribute all of its profits as earned income, and is then liquidated with significant reserves on which Entrepreneurs' Relief/Business Asset Disposal Relief is claimed at only 10%, potentially for this to happen on a "rinse and repeat" cycle every few years.

The government's response has been to amend tax law so that a capital distribution on a voluntary liquidation of a close company may later be re-categorised as an income distribution – a dividend – and then re-taxed more heavily, where a director/shareholder in that company ends up carrying on a similar activity within two years of that liquidation. This retrospective measure can be applied even where a liquidator has been appointed.

This may again be a concern particularly for property developers, who often like to keep each of their construction projects in separate companies, either because it minimises financial risk if a particular project "goes bad", or because they have different co-investors for different projects (or both). The rules to counter phoenixing are complex and their application far from certain, but they do include a "tax-motivated arrangements" requirement in order to be triggered, and the government has said that companies undertaking ordinary commercial transactions should **not** be affected.

16.7. Dying in Harness and/or Living Off the Profits

Many businessmen take the view that their company is their pension, and as such, they have no plans to liquidate or sell. Instead, the company will pay them dividends which they will live on in their retirement.

> **Case Study - 36   Living Off the Profits – Patience is a Virtue**
>
> Sana had a modest property portfolio in a company that she owns 100%. She had a good job, and so was able, over the years, to allow the profits to roll up in the company without having to take much out to supplement her income needs. Born in December 1955, she decided to retire both from work and as a landlady. She was eligible for State Pension from age 66, in December 2022. Once the company had sold its properties and paid off its Corporation Tax by mid-2024 it had £500,000 in liquid funds.
>
> Let's assume that Sana is a Higher Rate taxpayer in 2024/25, and paid a nominal amount to set up the company, many years ago. Let us also assume that her State Pension and private pensions will provide her with £20,000 income per year.
>
> Sana has a choice:
>
> 1. If she liquidates the company in 2024/25, she will pay £5,000 in professional fees to liquidate the company and, on the basis that her shares cost practically nothing when she set the company up, a CGT bill of (£495,000 – £3,000) @ 20% = £98,400.
>
>   So she will have a little under £400,000 left over out of her £500,000 company.
>
> 2. Alternatively, she can keep the company going with its funds invested appropriately, and take a second 'pension' of £30,000 in dividends every year, at a personal tax cost of c£2,600 a year (thanks to her pre-existing pensions, etc.). Assuming that any investment income earned by the company will cover the modest costs of running a dormant company, that second pension will last around 16 years, and cost around £41,000 in Income Tax over that entire period – about 40% of what it would have cost to extract the funds as a capital sum immediately in 2024/25.
>
> Note that Option 2 will **not** trigger the anti-avoidance legislation at 16.6.3 above because it is already being taxed as an income distribution – a dividend.
>
> Not only is Option 2 potentially much more efficient than Option 1, but it is also potentially much more efficient than if Sana had run her business personally –

unincorporated. If we suppose that Sana was already a Higher-Rate taxpayer prior to retirement:

1. Sana could have paid Income Tax at 40% or even 45% on these profits while working, but instead paid only 19% Corporation Tax (assuming post-2023 profits were no more than £50,000pa);

2. The additional tax to get the company's money into Sana's hands via dividends is currently 8.75% meaning that, even after the "double tax charge", (see 4.4), Sana's overall effective tax rate is only 26% - little more than half what she might have suffered as an Additional Rate taxpayer.

    To put things another way, an annual gross income of £30,000 while an Additional Rate taxpayer – while Sana was working – would have cost her £13,500pa, leaving only £16,500 after tax. By keeping the business in a company and suffering personal tax only when she actually wanted the money after retirement, Sana is effectively paying only £7,826pa for her £30,000 "annual pension", and that figure includes the Corporation Tax paid while allowing profits to roll up in the company.

Of course Sana's tax projections assume that the Higher Rate Threshold will not fall below £50,000, and that the personal tax on dividend income below that Threshold will remain at 8.75% over the next decade or so. But if the Income Tax on dividends *does* rise significantly a few years down the line, she could potentially take the CGT route on the funds remaining in the company at that point, and she should still be better off overall.

This may be a reasonable strategy, but it is important to take account of another tax that we have not yet looked at – Inheritance Tax.

Perhaps appropriately, one of the final chapters of this guide deals with this.

17. Inheritance Tax and Companies

Most explanations of Inheritance Tax ("IHT") begin with a weak joke about "death and taxes", but it is important to realise that IHT is not only a tax on death. In a number of situations, it can be payable during your lifetime.

This guide is not the place for a detailed study of all the IHT planning techniques, but in this chapter, I want to look at some examples of how IHT interacts with property companies.

17.1. IHT – the Basics

IHT is charged on "transfers of value". The commonest "transfer of value" is a gift, but as we shall see, there are other things which, sometimes unexpectedly, are transfers of value.

On basic principles, IHT is charged when an individual makes a transfer that reduces the value of their Estate – say by giving away money, or deliberately selling a property at under-value to a friend or relative. So, all such gifts, etc., may be triggers for IHT, although most are ignored during one's lifetime, as they will be treated as Potentially Exempt Transfers – PETs (see 17.4)

When a person dies, they are charged to IHT as if they had made a transfer of value of everything they owned on the day they died. In addition, any transfers of value they made in the seven years ending on the date they died are included in the assessment of the value of their chargeable Estate on death.

IHT is charged at the following rates for 2024/25, depending on whether the transfer of value was made during a person's lifetime, or on his or her death:

Transfer of value	Death Rate	Lifetime Rate
0 – 325,000	0%	0%
Above 325,000	40%	20%

17.2. Nil Rate Band (NRB)

The first £325,000, which is charged at 0%, is called the Nil Rate Band ("NRB"). It is often referred to as an "exemption", but this is a misleading way to think about it, as we shall see. Each individual has his or her own NRB. The NRB is scheduled to remain at £325,000 until 2028. The NRB was first pegged at £325,000 in 2009 – 15 years ago now, since when property prices have almost doubled.

Transfers to one's spouse or civil partner *are* exempt, and do not use up the deceased's NRB. Basically, if a person leaves everything to their surviving spouse, then there will be no IHT. This used to mean that the deceased's NRB was then wasted but, **since 2007, the surviving spouse also acquires any NRB that the deceased has not already used against gifts, etc., to other parties.** This means that it is much easier to ensure that both NRBs available to a couple are fully utilised, and it is quite common now to see the second or surviving spouse or civil partner have £650,000 (2 x NRB) available on his or her death (where everything was left to the surviving spouse on first death).

17.3. Residence Nil Rate Band (RNRB)

This is a relatively new measure, available only on death (unlike the standard NRB, which is also available to cover chargeable lifetime transfers), available with effect from 2017/18, as follows:

- £100,000 in 2017/18
- £125,000 in 2018/19
- £150,000 in 2019/20
- £175,000 in 2020/21 (again, pegged to 2027/28 in the 2022 Autumn Statement)

It is available to cover value in the deceased's home, provided it is transferred to direct descendants (children, grandchildren, etc.). It can cover only the value in the main home, so can be wasted if the value of the deceased's interest in his home falls short of the RNRB available. Like the 'ordinary' NRB, it is available to each individual, so a couple will have one each.

It follows that, since 2020/21, a couple potentially has had access to:

2 x (£325,000 + £175,000) = £1million in combined (R)NRBs.

Like the standard NRB, the RNRB is transferrable between spouses; it is possible also to transfer wealth *equivalent* to the home, rather than the property itself, if (for example) the deceased had to go into care prior to death, and the former home had been sold. However, that value equivalent to the RNRB being claimed must still be transferred to direct descendants, in order to qualify. But, simply put, it does mean that there may well be more standard NRB left over to cover other assets, such as valuable company shareholdings – so long as the home itself does not use up all of the available nil rate bands.

Aside from having to ensure that value equivalent to the RNRB being claimed passes only to direct descendants, another key difference between the RNRB and the 'normal' NRB is that the RNRB can be tapered away if the chargeable value of the deceased's estate exceeds £2million. (Note that the chargeable value is net of liabilities, such as mortgages). The taper rate is 50%, meaning that the RNRB is reduced by £1 for every £2 by which the deceased's net estate exceeds £2million.

Case Study - 37   Basic NRB and RNRB Calculations

Donald is a wealthy property investor, holding shares in his property company worth £1m, together with a half-share in a palatial residence. Unfortunately, he is taken far too soon in a freak sunbed accident in 2020; his Will leaves everything, including his share in the family home, to his wife, Melissa. There is no IHT on Donald's death, because he has left everything to his spouse. She will acquire Donald's NRB and RNRB, as he has used neither.

When Melissa dies in 2025, she leaves everything (including her home) to her son, Brandon; neither Donald nor Melissa made any lifetime transfers in the 7 years prior to their deaths.

Value of shares at death	£1,200,000
Add: value of home	£1,300,000
Total	£2,500,000
Deduct NRB x 2	(650,000)
RNRB x 2 £350,000 BUT: RNRB Taper - ½ x (£2.5m - £2m) = £250,000 Residual RNRB	(100,000)
Taxable	1,750,000
IHT Payable (40%)	**700,000**

IHT calculations are almost invariably far more complicated than the above example, but it does illustrate the basics maths of the NRB and RNRB. Melissa does not acquire Donald's NRB and RNRB that applied on his death, but his unused proportion (in this case 100%) of the Bands that are in point, when she later dies.

17.4. PETs

Not all transfers of value attract IHT when they are made. **A simple gift from one individual, during his or her lifetime, to another individual will be a "potentially exempt transfer" ("PET").** This means that if the individual making the gift lives for another seven years after making it, it will fall out of account and no IHT will be charged on it when the individual dies. If, however, they die within seven years, it will form part of their estate at death.

> **Case Study - 38   A Failed PET**
>
> Joe is a middle aged widower. On 1 April 2023, he makes a cash gift to his son of £100,000, to help him buy a house. This is a PET for IHT purposes, and so there is no IHT to pay at the time. Sadly, during 2024, Joe is killed in a car crash. His estate at death, after deducting all debts, is worth £250,000.

Because Joe has not survived for seven years after making the gift to his son, the PET is added to his estate when calculating the IHT:

Value of estate at death	250,000
Add gifts in last seven years	100,000
Total	350,000
Deduct NRB	(325,000)
Chargeable to IHT at 40%	25,000

Note that, if Joe had survived the cash gift to his son by more than 3 years, then the IHT due on the gift would be tapered. (The more years between gift and death, the greater the taper – the taper is effectively 100% after 7 years).

*The Residence Nil Rate Band would be fully in point by 2024: let's assume that Joe acquired his late wife's RNRB in full on her death, (but she had bequeathed £325,000 of her other assets to the children of a previous marriage, so had no NRB left to transfer to Joe) and he also left his home worth exactly 2 x £175,000 = £350,000 to their son so it has been exactly 100% utilised. It has therefore been left out of account both in terms of the value of the chargeable Estate and the corresponding reliefs, to make the above example as simple as possible

17.5. Gift with Reservation of Benefit

A gift is only a PET if it is really given away. If the person making the gift continues to enjoy a benefit from it, it will be a **"gift with reservation of benefit. ("GWROB")**. It will be treated as still being owned by the giver. The commonest example of a GWROB is where a parent gifts their house to their child, but continues to live there; however, any gift that the giver continues to enjoy will be a GWROB:

Case Study - 39   GWROB

Sue is a widow, getting on in years, and like many otherwise modestly-off people, she has one hugely valuable asset – her house. It is worth £350,000, and the mortgage was paid off long ago. The rest of her assets come to £200,000.

She makes a gift of the house to her two children, but continues to live in it. Ten years later she dies, still living in the house.

Because she "reserved a benefit" in the house, by continuing to live in it, for IHT purposes she is treated as if she still owned the house, so the value of her death estate includes the value of the house at the time of her death. It is irrelevant that she has survived for over seven years since she gave the house away – for IHT purposes it is still hers.

The GWROB rules were sometimes easy to get around, despite numerous tweaks to the legislation over the years. New rules were introduced more than a decade ago, that tried to encompass GWROB scenarios. The effect of the relatively new "Pre-Owned Assets Tax" regime is that, if for some reason you are able to circumvent the GWROB regime, then you should – usually, but not always – be subjected to an annual Income Tax charge, broadly based on the rental value of any asset that you continue to enjoy, having legally given it away. The rules for "GWROB" and "POAT" can be complex, particularly in their interaction with each other, and will happily catch innocent transactions where no avoidance was intended or realised. If you think that the rules may apply, then you should get advice.

17.6. Spouse Exemption

A gift or a legacy from one spouse or civil partner to the other is exempt from IHT. If you die and leave everything absolutely to your spouse, there will be no IHT to pay, and when they die, they can use double the Nil Rate Band (and, potentially, Residence Nil Rate Band) at the time of their death: both theirs and yours (because you have not used yours up, if you leave everything to your spouse).

This becomes more complicated – more restricted – if one spouse or civil partner is **not** "domiciled" in a UK jurisdiction – typically where they were born to parents who were not themselves of UK "origin"; even so, the surviving spouse usually now has the option to elect to be treated as UK-domiciled, to similar effect.

17.7. Business Property Relief

For IHT purposes, "business property" gets relief at either 50% or 100%, depending on its nature. The crucial types of business property for property investors are:

- An interest in a business (that is, a sole trader, or a partner)

- Shares in an unlisted **trading** company

Both these can qualify for 100% BPR, and thus effectively escape IHT, but it is crucial to bear in mind that a "business" or a "trading company" does **NOT** in this context include a business that substantively involves:

- Making or holding investments – and HMRC regard property letting as falling into this category

- Dealing in land – although a property development company **may** qualify as long as it is predominantly "developing" property – new builds or major refurbishments – and not simply buying and selling land and/or properties

Most property *investment* companies, therefore, are unlikely to qualify for Business Property Relief, and so the planning for them will tend to involve making gifts of property assets and/or shares during one's lifetime, and hoping to survive at least seven years.

But **many property *development* companies will qualify for BPR**, so the shares in such companies should pass free of IHT to the intended beneficiaries – children, grandchildren, etc.

Simply put, if a company is involved in both property development and property letting, then its shares may qualify for 100% BPR despite the non-trading letting part, so long as that is clearly the subsidiary part of a predominantly trading company – in this case, property development.

However, "surplus" assets that broadly have no current or future purpose in the business may be "excepted" from BPR – there will be no BPR relief on the value of the excepted asset. (Note that this differs in operation to the "all or nothing" approach to whether a company is predominantly trading, or predominantly holding or making investments, as above: in *that* scenario, the shares either qualify for BPR or they do not). The intention of the excepted assets rule is to ensure that there is no benefit in "stuffing" non-business or private assets into an otherwise-qualifying company.

So, for example, HMRC will be keen to ascertain if there is any excess cash that is clearly surplus to requirements, to restrict the BPR available. But if the funds are instead demonstrably required for future business expansion, with evidence of negotiations to buy land for development, or planning permission sought for a new project, then that cash may be treated as part of the company's qualifying business assets.

This guide is not the place to look at detailed planning strategies to minimise IHT, but rather to give a sense of the principles involved – this is a huge subject, and there is probably no area of taxation where skilled professional advice is more ESSENTIAL to avoid pitfalls.

Caution

It is not an exaggeration to say that any layman who attempts to do IHT planning more sophisticated than leaving everything to his (or her) spouse is likely to produce unexpected and expensive results for himself and his family.

Even leaving everything to your spouse or civil partner could be a mistake.

17.8. Close Companies and IHT

IHT is mainly a tax on individuals (and Trusts), and there is a common misconception that it cannot apply to companies. This is generally the case, but there are exceptions:

Case Study - 40   Transfer of Value by a Close Company

Mr Smart is a widower and the sole owner of a property investment company. The value of his 100 £1 shares is £1million. Mindful of the IHT consequences if he dies still owning all of it (no BPR, so fully chargeable to IHT), he wants to give half the company to his son (who is not involved with the company, having a full time job of his own).

He knows that if he simply gifts 50 shares to his son, he will be treated as having sold them for market value and will pay CGT on £500,000, (see for example 16.4.8), so he comes up with another idea – he gets his son to subscribe for 100 new shares, paying their face value of £1 each. His son should therefore own half of the shares then in issue.

Unfortunately, this is one of those rare examples where a close company can be involved in a transfer of value for IHT.

Because his son paid much less than market value for the shares, the shareholders before the shares were issued (here, Mr Smart) have suffered a loss in wealth and are treated as having made a transfer of value for IHT – and this type of transfer is not a gift from one individual to another, so it cannot be a PET.

It is immediately chargeable to IHT at the lifetime rate of 20%.

The amount of the transfer is the amount by which Mr Smart's estate has reduced in value, not the amount received by his son, so it is not £499,900 (the difference between the value of the shares and the amount he paid the company for them). In fact in this case, it is worse. To work out how bad, we need to look at the effect on Mr Smart:

The value of each share before the issue to his son was £10,000 (1,000,000 divided by 100).

After the share issue, Mr Smart no longer has absolute control of the company, because he only has half the shares and cannot outvote his son if there is a dispute.

It is normal to discount the value of the shares by around 20% (it would have been more for a trading company) to reflect the fact that the shareholder has less than absolute control over the underlying assets in the company.

The value of Mr Smart's 100 shares is therefore £500,000 (half the value of the whole company), less £100,000 (20% discount for loss of control of his company), so his shares are now worth £400,000. His transfer of value is therefore:

Value of 100 shares (100% of company) before share issue	1,000,000
Less value of 100 shares (now just 50% of company) after share issue – having lost overall control of company	(400,000)
Deemed transfer of value	600,000
Less NRB (no previous gifts)	(325,000)
Chargeable to IHT at 20% (lifetime rate)	275,000
IHT payable	55,000

Note – because of the way IHT is calculated on transfers like this, the actual amount might be somewhat different, but for simplicity, £55,000 gives a good idea of the amount due.

> This is a rude introduction to one of IHT's most important 'lessons': **it is not the value of the asset transferred that is important, so much as the effect it has on your estate**: giving away even a small shareholding in a company – where it means you lose a controlling majority interest – can mean a big IHT bill. Mr. Smart can console himself that he is by no means the first taxpayer – or adviser – to fall foul of this key principle.
>
> It does not end there – there is anti-avoidance legislation for CGT, which means that Mr Smart is treated as having made a disposal for CGT purposes of £500,000, by "value shifting" (see Case Study - 16)
>
> Fortunately for him, however, because the transfer was immediately chargeable to IHT, he can "hold over" this gain, in much the same way as he could have done if the shares had been shares in a trading company.

The above example was a disaster for Mr Smart, because he did not realise the IHT he would have to pay, but in fact much IHT planning for property investment companies revolves around deliberately incurring IHT "charges" (but usually, carefully kept within the £325,000 Nil Rate Band so as not to have to actually pay any IHT) as a way of holding over the capital gain on a gift of the shares.

We do not want you to get lost in the detail on IHT planning for property companies – it really is a case of "don't try this at home" – but we hope you will realise from the above that IHT cannot be ignored by owners of property companies, even though they may not be around when the time comes to pay the tax!

To end on a piece of good news – IHT is normally payable (broadly) six months after the transfer of value (or the date of death), but where it is charged on property deriving its value from land, it is often possible to arrange to pay the tax in ten annual instalments – the idea being that the property should **not** need to be sold off to pay the IHT.

Good Advisors Do Save You TAX!

This section has been written by Amer Siddiq, founder of www.property-tax-portal.co.uk.

18. Finding an Accountant

There is a saying, "a good accountant pays for him/herself". Never a truer word has been spoken.

In this chapter we will become familiar with and understand how to acquire the services of an excellent accountant.

18.1. Accountancy Qualifications

The first step is to ensure that your accountant is a member of a recognised institute.

Some of the popular ones amongst accountants are ACA, ACCA, ICAEW, ICAS etc.

Here is what these abbreviations stand for:

- Association of Chartered Accountants (ACA)
- Association of Chartered Certified Accountants (ACCA)
- Institute of Chartered Accountants in England and Wales (ICAEW)
- Institute of Chartered Accountants in Scotland (ICAS)

Furthermore, it would not be a bad idea to pick an accountant who is a member of the Chartered Institute of Taxation or Association of Taxation Technicians.

Getting to know the history of your proposed accountant is a very good idea, so look for the following signs:

a) Are they a former Tax Inspector?
b) Have they passed the Taxation (ATII/CTA, ATT) exams?

A qualified tax advisor is useful for all sorts of tax related services and these include:

- Preparing tax returns
- Sole trader tax returns
- Tax planning advice

It is most likely that your tax advisor will charge on an hourly basis. However, some will agree a flat fee beforehand.

It is pertinent to ask whether one should go for a general or specialist tax advisor, although it may seem better to go with the general advisor as he/she will most definitely be cheaper.

However, in the long-term the specialist may save you money because of his/her in depth knowledge and experience.

18.2. General Advisor or Tax Specialist?

A specialist will have the answer, usually to hand, whereas a non-specialist may have to consult HMRC documentation or may indeed consult the specialist and then pass the charge back on to you.

Cost can be a significant issue, as a specialist can charge around £270 per hour. For this you get about 15 minutes of quizzing followed by 45 minutes' worth of (in most cases) written response (Oh and that's plus VAT!)

To put that into perspective a non-specialist can charge around £150 per hour. A typical session with a non-specialist can take up to 2.5 hours. This time would be typically spent in the following way:

- 15 minutes of clarification.
- 1.5 hours of research.
- 45 minutes of written response.

As you can see sometimes it is beneficial if you go direct to a specialist, particularly if your questions to your accountant require him/her to study before responding.

With the above two examples in mind it is important to ascertain a working relationship with your advisor. You should be familiar with his/her area of expertise and know what their limitations are i.e. what they are not too hot on.

18.3. How to Choose Your Adviser

Before you sign up with a tax adviser or accountant, be sure to address the following:

18.3.1. Will I Need a Tax Adviser or an Accountant?

More often than not people will actually require both, however, it is important to establish why you need them - do you need someone to manage your accounts and help you with your tax return, or someone to give you sound advice that will legally save you money. Your accountant can manage your accounts, provide compliance work, and some may even do tax planning.

However, tax advisers tend to focus solely on tax planning. They spend significant amounts of time keeping up-to-date with the latest tax legislation and tax cases to help make sure they provide their clients with great strategies that will help to reduce or eliminate tax - some of which your accountant may not even be aware of!

If we compare the accountancy profession with medicine, an accountant is the equivalent of a GP, and most of the time a GP is all you need for routine health care, but if you get seriously ill (compare with a dispute with HM Revenue and Customs) or you need surgery (tax planning), then you need a specialist consultant (a Tax Adviser).

18.3.2. What Qualifications?

As a client you want to be assured that your tax adviser / accountant is acting in both your best interest and within the law, which is why it is important to know what qualifications your tax adviser or accountant has, and when they were achieved and if they are relevant to you. Check that the qualifications they have cover the area of taxation or accounting that you require assistance with.

18.3.3. How Much Experience do they Have?

When choosing a tax adviser or accountant, it is good to know just how much experience they have and what their reputation is.

Do not be afraid to ask how long have they been giving advice, where they worked before or if they have ever done any public speaking or written work that you can refer back to? Another good question to ask is how many existing clients they have within the area that you are interested in, for example – if you develop property, how many other developers have they provided advice for and will they be able to provide references?

Good advisers will boast about their success, so give them the opportunity to do so!

18.3.4. How Much Will It Cost?

That really does depend on what type of advice or service you require. The fees generally reflect the adviser's / accountant's level of experience and qualifications, along with the amount of time they may have to spend on your case; in this instance you can request an estimate of the total. Also ask when fees need to be paid by.

Some accountants and tax advisers do offer 'fixed fees' for certain types of advice or help so that you know exactly what you are paying and exactly what you will receive.

Try to negotiate a fixed fee wherever possible, as good advisers won't be afraid to operate on this basis. It is far better than the 'let the clock run' approach, though in some cases such as a tax investigation, hourly charges are the only practical way to work.

18.3.5. Professional Bodies

There are various professional bodies that you will find tax advisers and accountants to be part of.

Anybody who claims to be able to give 'tax advice' should be a 'Chartered Tax Adviser' (CTA), which means that they will be a member of the Chartered Institute of Taxation and will have taken and passed their examinations.

Qualified accountants will have Chartered Certified Accountant (ACCA or FCCA), or Chartered Accountant (CA, ACA or FCA) in their title.

18.3.6. What About Indemnity Cover?

If an adviser gives you inappropriate advice or your accountant does not manage your accounts correctly it could result in a huge financial loss for you.

Finding out at the beginning what indemnity cover a tax adviser or accountant has will mean peace of mind for you. Find out whether they are covered for loss of documents, court attendance and legal fees, breach of confidence or misuse of information to suggest just a few areas. Ask who they are covered by and for how much per claim.

Knowing what protection your adviser or accountant has will protect you. You will be alarmed to learn that some advisers do not even have indemnity cover and you are well advised to stay away from such advisers. Chartered accountants and Chartered Tax Advisers are required by the rules of their professional bodies to have professional indemnity insurance.

18.3.7. *How do I Contact My Tax Adviser / Accountant?*

It can be quite frustrating when each time you phone your tax adviser or accountant they are unavailable.

Find out in advance how to contact them and if this suits you.

If you have 'ad-hoc' questions to ask your adviser or accountant and you cannot reach them, how soon will they get back to you? Also, find out if they are happy to receive email as you may prefer this method of correspondence.

Your chosen advisers should personally respond to your enquiries and calls within an agreed timescale.

A recent development has been the growth of online accountants and tax advisers, and if you do not feel the need for face to face contact with your adviser, you may want to consider using such a firm. Having lower overheads in the form of offices and meeting rooms, they are often able to offer lower fees than the conventional firms.

18.3.8. *Keep up to Date with Tax Legislation Changes*

Tax legislation is constantly changing. That is why it is important that your adviser or accountant keeps up-to-date with all the changes.

Also, to retain their qualifications, tax advisers and accountants must adhere to on-going training programmes enforced by their regulatory bodies, to ensure that they are keeping abreast of the latest changes in legislation and the latest tax planning opportunities.

For example, CPD (Continuing Professional Development) is the compulsory training a Chartered Tax Adviser is required to do each year in order to keep his qualifications. Basically, this requires a minimum of 90 hours' training per year, between "structured" training - that is, attending seminars, lectures, etc., and "unstructured" training (such as reading textbooks and technical articles)

18.3.9. *What if I Have an Emergency?*

You are now aware of how to contact your tax adviser or accountant, but what happens if you have an emergency and need urgent tax advice?

How available are they in a crisis?

Knowing that you can rely on the tax adviser or accountant is an important point when considering their services. Make sure that you are able to contact them without having to arrange a formal meeting!

18.3.10. *Does the Adviser Sell 'Off the Shelf' Packages?*

This is a very important question to ask your adviser. There are certain advisers out there who sell tax schemes (also known as 'off the shelf' tax solutions) and earn significant amounts of commission by doing so.

"Tax Schemes" come in all sorts of forms – one example (now stopped by legislation) was the creation of artificial capital losses to set against capital gains.

If your adviser mentions such schemes to you, then be cautious as HM Revenue and Customs are getting tough on such schemes, and legislation has been introduced requiring those using them to disclose the fact to HMRC.

19. The Importance of Tax Planning

This section has been written by Amer Siddiq, founder of www.property-tax-portal.co.uk.

We all instinctively do some tax planning in our daily lives, even if it is simply remembering to buy our "duty frees" when we return from our holiday abroad.

If you are going to make the best of your property business, then you need to be alert to the tax implications of your business plans, and to any opportunities to reduce the likely tax bill. Your instinct may be enough for your duty free goodies, but for tax on your business, you need a more structured approach!

"Tax planning" means arranging your business affairs so that you pay the minimum amount of tax that the law requires. It does not mean trying to conceal things from the Taxman, and it does not mean indulging in highly complex (and expensive!) artificial "tax avoidance" schemes.

"Every man is entitled if he can to order his affairs so that the tax attaching under the appropriate Acts is less than it would otherwise be." That is what the House of Lords said in 1935, when they found for the Duke of Westminster and against the Inland Revenue. This still holds true today, though there is now a mass of "anti-avoidance" legislation to consider when thinking about tax planning – and before you ask, the Duke's tax planning idea was stopped by anti-avoidance legislation!

19.1. Knowing When to Consider Planning

A question you will most certainly ask yourself is "when should I consider tax planning for my property business?"

The short answer is "all the time", but to be realistic, no-one is likely to do this. The trick is to develop by experience, a sense of when a tax planning opportunity (or a potentially expensive tax pitfall) is likely to present itself.

You should consider tax planning in all of the following situations, for example:

19.1.1. Buying

If you are buying a property, you need to consider:

- Buying the property – It could be you as an individual, you and your spouse, you and a business partner, a Limited Company owned by you, or perhaps a Trust you have set up. Your decision will depend on your future business strategy

- Financing the property – You will need to consider whether you are taking out a mortgage, and if so how will it be secured. It may not always make sense to secure the loan on the property you are buying if you have other assets on which you can secure the loan.

- Plans for the property – It could be that you are you buying the property to sell it again in the short term, or to hold it long term and benefit from the rental income. The tax treatment will be different according to which is the case, and different planning should be done before the property is bought.

19.1.2. Repairs and Refurbishment

If you spend money on a property, you need to consider:

- Whether you are doing it in order to sell it again in the short term, or whether you will continue letting it.

- If the work being done is classed as a **repair** to the property, or an **improvement.** See below for the difference between the two.

The distinction between a repair and an improvement to a property is very important, because although the cost of repairs can be deducted from your rental income for tax purposes, an improvement can only be claimed as a deduction against CGT when you sell the property.

Essentially, a repair is when you replace like with like, whereas an improvement involves adding to the property (say, a conservatory or a loft conversion), or replacing a thing with something significantly better (say, removing the old storage heaters and installing oil-fired central heating).

HMRC do not always behave logically when it comes to repairs versus improvements.

A taxpayer sold a seaside property, in circumstances where he would have to pay CGT on the sale profit. He had spent a lot of money on this property, which when he bought it had not been touched since the early 1950s.

He had ripped out the old "utility" kitchen, for example, and replaced it with a state-of-the-art designer affair in gleaming slate, chrome and steel. The old 1950s cooker had had some Bakelite knobs to turn the gas on and off – the new kitchen range had the computer power of the average 1970s space capsule.

Clearly an improvement, and so deductible from his capital gain, but HMRC tried to argue that one kitchen is much like another and he was just replacing like with like – so they said it was a repair, which was no good to him in his case as there was no rental income from which he could deduct the cost of repairs.

19.1.3. Selling

When you decide to dispose of a property, there are other tax issues to consider:

- Who is the property going to? – If it is to someone "connected" with you, such as a close relative or a business partner, and if you do not charge them the full market value, HMRC can step in and tax you as if you had sold it for full value.

- Will you be paying CGT or income tax on the profit you make? – The planning opportunities are very different, depending on which tax is involved.

- What are the terms of the sale? Is it just a cash sale, or is the buyer a developer who is offering you a "slice of the action" in the form of a share of the profits from the development? There is important anti-avoidance legislation to consider if this is the case.

19.1.4. Life changes

Whenever your life undergoes some significant changes, you should consider tax planning.

Here are some examples when tax planning should be considered:

- Getting married – a married couple (and a civil partnership) have a number of tax planning opportunities denied to single people, but there are also one or two pitfalls to watch out for.

- Moving house – it is usually not a good idea to sell the old house immediately, as there are often tax advantages to keeping it and letting it out.

- Changing your job. You may become a higher or lower rate taxpayer and this may mean you should change your tax strategy.

    If you are moving house, and you sell the old residence, you will have the cash left after you have paid off the mortgage and the various removal costs to spend on your new home. If you need a mortgage to buy the new home, the interest on that mortgage is not allowed as a deduction for tax purposes.

    If, instead, you re-mortgage the old house and let it out, ALL of the mortgage interest you pay can be deducted against the rent you receive (subject to partial restriction as per Chapter 6) whatever you do with the cash you have released.

- Death – IHT is charged at 40% on the value of your estate when you die, to the extent that the value is greater than (for 2024/25) £325,000 – as potentially enhanced by the Residence Nil Rate Band, and/or spouses, civil partners, etc (see Chapter 17). By planning early enough it is possible to reduce the IHT burden considerably.

19.1.5. Politics

There are two occasions each year when you need to be particularly alert – the Budget in November or December, and The Spring Statement in March or April.

On both these occasions the Chancellor of the Exchequer announces tax rates, and new tax legislation, which might well affect you and your property business. In some cases, however, new tax legislation is announced at other times – it pays to keep a weather eye on the financial pages of the newspaper, or to subscribe to a magazine or journal that will alert you to important tax changes that may affect your business.

19.1.6. End and Start of Tax Year

The tax year ends on the 5th April each year and it is a good idea to review your tax situation before this date to make sure you are not missing any planning opportunities.

19.2. The Real Benefits of Tax Planning

Robert Kiyosaki, author of the number one bestselling book 'Rich Dad Poor Dad', says *'Every time people try to punish the rich, the rich don't simply comply, they react. They have the money, power and intent to change things. They do not sit there and voluntarily pay more taxes. They search for ways to minimize their tax burden'*

The whole purpose of tax planning is to save you tax and to put more profits in your pocket. That is why the rich are always looking at ways of beating the taxman, because they benefit from tax planning.

19.2.1. *Paying Less Tax*

Don't fall into the trap where you only think about tax when you are considering selling or even worse after you have sold the property.

By taking tax advice at the right times and on a regular basis you will legitimately avoid or reduce taxes both in the short and the long term.

This means that you will have greater profits to spend as you wish.

19.2.2. *Clear 'Entrance' and 'Exit' Strategies*

When you sit down and analyse properties that you are considering for investment, you will no doubt look at how much rental income the property will generate and what you expect to achieve in capital appreciation.

Knowing the estimated tax liabilities right from the outset will save you from any nasty surprises in the future.

> Your personal circumstances can change at a whim. The last thing that you want to do is fall into a situation where you are forced to sell a property but are unable to pay the taxman because you never considered your tax situation.

19.2.3. *Staying Focused*

When you are deciding on the property investment strategies that you are going to adopt it is a good idea to talk them through with a tax adviser.

If your investment strategy changes then it is likely to have an impact on your tax strategy, so it should be reviewed with your tax adviser.

Your tax strategy will go hand in hand with your investment strategy and will help you to keep focused on your property investment and financial goals.

19.2.4. *Improving Cash Flow*

One of the challenges that you will face as a property investor is cash flow. In other words, you need to make sure that you have enough money coming in from your property business to pay for all property related bills, maintenance and repairs, and of course tax on the rental profits.

> Remember, timing of expenditures can be the difference between a 'high' and a 'nil' tax bill. Therefore, keeping in regular contact with your tax adviser, especially when coming towards the end of the tax year, can have a significant impact on your property cash flow.

19.2.5. Avoiding Common Tax Traps

There are many tax traps that you can fall into if you have not taken any tax advice at all, not to mention the numerous great tax planning opportunities you will miss out on too.

It is not uncommon to hear stories about investors who have made a £100,000 profit on a single property and then sold it without taking any tax advice whatsoever. If you fall into this situation, then you could be facing a tax bill of up to £45,000.

It will hurt you even more if after selling you realise that you could have easily turned the tax liability to zero had you taken some simple tax advice.

Good tax advisers will know of the most common traps that you are likely to fall into, so a few minutes spent wisely could save you thousands in taxes.

19.3. The Golden Tax Rules

The challenge to you as a property investor will no doubt be how to grow a profitable portfolio. One of the easiest ways you can make money in property is to pay less tax.

19.3.1. Education…Education…Education

Whether you are starting out in property investing or are an experienced landlord with a sizeable portfolio, there is one thing that you should always do - educate yourself to make sure you are:

a) complying with the ever changing legal requirements

b) learning how to make your investments more profitable

c) making sure you keep up-to-date with tax changes that may affect your tax liability.

Although there is never a substitute for taking professional advice, you should keep yourself updated so that you can discuss these opportunities with your adviser at your next appointment.

19.3.2. Prevention is Better Than Cure

There is a proverb 'prevention is better than cure' (believe it or not this was first said by the famous medieval philosopher Erasmus) and he probably was not thinking about tax when he said it, but it most certainly applies.

Planning for a tax situation you are likely to face is much better than trying to get out of a tax problem that you have unknowingly (or even knowingly) fallen into. It is certain that trying to get out of a tax problem will cost much more in specialist/consultancy fees and there is never a guarantee that you will get out of the problem.

20. Appendix A – Template Documents

On the following two pages you will find template documents that you can use.

Examples of these documents once filled in are given in section 7.4.

The two documents are as follows:

- Meeting Minute
- Dividend Confirmation

Meeting Minute

Name of Company: _____

Company Registration No: _____

Address: _____

_____

_____

Minutes of a Meeting of the Board of Directors

Date of the meeting held at the Registered Office of the Company: ___/___/___

Present:

_____   _____

_____   _____

DIVIDENDS

It was resolved that the company pay an interim dividend in respect of the period ending ___/___/___ to holders registered as at ___/___/___ as follows:

Share Class	Dividend Rate	Date to be Paid
Ordinary of _____	_____ per share	___/___/___

ANY OTHER BUSINESS:

_____

_____

Signed on Behalf of the Board

Name_____   Date: ___/___/___   Position: _____

Dividend Confirmation

Name of Company: _____
Company Registration No: _____

Address: _____

_____

Dividend Confirmation

Interim dividend for the period ending ___/___/___ to shareholders registered on ___/___/___

Payment Date
___/___/___

Shareholder Details
_____ _____
_____ _____
_____ _____

Shareholding	Dividend Rate	Dividend Payment
_____Ordinary shares of_____	____ **per share**	£_____

This dividend confirmation should be kept as part of your financial records.

_____
(company secretary)
___/___/___

Date:

Page - 145

21. Appendix B – Tables

Note: throughout these tables, and unlike previous versions of this book, we have dispensed with the assumption that there is a fixed £1,000 additional cost to the corporate route, in terms of extra accountancy and professional fees, bank charges and administration costs in dealing with the additional compliance work required in order to run a company. As the margins between the standard unincorporated route and the incorporated model become slimmer, the previous adjustment to include a substantial fixed sum is considered now to be too unwieldy, to the point of being potentially quite distortive.

But it does mean that readers will need to accommodate some reasonably tailored adjustment for the "corporate overhead", in their thinking.

21.1. Comparing Individual Property Investor with a Company (2023/24 v 2024/25)

The following table looks at the potential savings (or costs) to an unincorporated landlord running his or her residential property investment business through a company instead.

	2023/24			2024/25		
Taxable Profit	Net Income as Individual Investor; Interest Cost = 33% of Profit	Net Income Through Company £12.5k* Salary	2023/24 Saving / (Cost) of Incorporation £12.5k* Salary; Interest Cost = 33% of Profit	Net Income as Individual Investor; Interest Cost = 33% of Profit	Net Income Through Company £12.5k* Salary	2024/25 Saving / (Cost) of Incorporation £12.5k* Salary; Interest Cost = 33% of Profit
-	-	-	-	-	-	-
10,000	10,000	9,810	(190)	10,000	9,810	(190)
15,000	14,514	14,097	(417)	14,514	14,054	(460)
20,000	18,514	17,793	(721)	18,514	17,749	(765)
25,000	22,514	21,489	(1,025)	22,514	21,445	(1,069)
30,000	26,514	25,184	(1,330)	26,514	25,141	(1,373)
35,000	30,514	28,880	(1,634)	30,514	28,836	(1,678)
40,000	33,928	32,576	(1,352)	33,928	32,532	(1,396)
45,000	36,598	36,271	(327)	36,598	36,227	(371)
50,000	39,268	39,967	699	39,268	39,923	655
55,000	41,938	43,662	1,724	41,938	43,619	1,681
60,000	44,608	47,276	2,668	44,608	47,232	2,624
70,000	49,948	52,295	2,347	49,948	52,252	2,304
80,000	54,008	57,165	3,157	54,008	57,121	3,113
90,000	56,688	62,034	5,346	56,688	61,990	5,302
100,000	60,547	66,903	6,356	60,547	66,860	6,313
110,000	65,222	71,773	6,551	65,222	71,729	6,507
120,000	69,897	76,642	6,745	69,897	76,598	6,701
130,000	74,572	81,003	6,431	74,572	80,959	6,387
140,000	79,247	84,219	4,972	79,247	84,175	4,928
150,000	83,922	87,434	3,512	83,922	87,391	3,469
160,000	88,597	90,650	2,053	88,597	90,606	2,009
170,000	93,272	94,970	1,698	93,272	94,926	1,654
180,000	97,947	99,428	1,481	97,947	99,384	1,437
190,000	102,622	103,886	1,264	102,622	103,842	1,220
200,000	107,297	108,343	1,046	107,297	108,300	1,003
250,000	130,672	130,632	(40)	130,672	130,588	(84)
300,000	154,047	153,258	(789)	154,047	153,214	(833)

*Salary of £9,000 when profits are only £10,000

The model assumes that the landlord is paying just under ¼ of his or her income out as residential mortgage interest (e.g., where rental profit *after* interest is £50,000, the interest cost is 33% of that income – i.e., c£16,667, which in turn represents 25% of gross income of £66,667 *before* interest is deducted).

Also assumed:

- Where interest is charged, interest costs are not fixed but are 33% of the net profit - £16,500 where net profits are £50,000, and £33,000 where net profits are £100,000
- The model assumes that in the company, the director/shareholder takes a small salary of £12,500 in both years, and then the entirety of the company's remaining profits as dividends
- The company has already used its Employment Allowance (or is a "singleton" director/shareholder company) so secondary NI Contributions will arise once earnings exceed the Secondary Earnings Threshold, as normal

Results and Comparisons

The table shows that incorporating the property business starts to be increasingly beneficial once the level of profits exceeds c£50,000 – broadly as the landlord's tax-adjusted income crosses the 40% Higher Rate threshold and the restriction to relief for residential finance costs starts to take effect. However, there is an upper limit to the net benefit of incorporation.

Once the Higher Rate Threshold is breached, the additional deemed taxable income (comprised in the interest added back) results in an *effective* marginal individual Income Tax rate that can significantly exceed the corresponding aggregate marginal net tax cost through a company, for the same increase in profits; where this occurs, running the business through a company is advantageous. Of course this *effective* rate is highly dependent on the scale or rate of interest being charged: the greater the interest, the more punitive the effective tax rate for the unincorporated individual.

This "saving" by incorporation is really only in comparison to the effective further cost of *not* incorporating, where residential property finance costs are significant. Once the taxpayer is being taxed as if he or she were a Higher Rate taxpayer, the net cost of getting only a 20% tax "credit" (reduction) instead of full tax relief on one's residential mortgage interest payments starts to become increasingly punitive as net profits and corresponding finance costs rise.

Broadly in line with the influence of tax relief for finance costs, the increased cost of Corporation Tax starts to apply when company profits exceed £50,000. However, the effect of the Corporation Tax hike is essentially in the opposite direction:

- Where residential property finance costs are significant, this makes the unincorporated route more expensive so that companies are comparably *more* attractive, while
- Higher Corporation Tax rates make the company route *less* attractive
- The 2024/25 result consistently shows a slight reduction in the benefit of incorporation of £44, reflecting the reduction in the "Dividend Allowance" from £1,000 in 2023/24 to just £500 in 2024/25.

Where the residential interest tax relief restriction is substantial, as here, there is still tangible benefit to incorporation in terms of minimising the overall annual Income Tax charge. But the range of profits and the extent of the net benefit may be narrowed.

Of course, just how punitive the restriction proves to be, depends on the extent of a given landlord's / landlady's residential property mortgage/finance costs, and where they are quite modest, then incorporation will be less attractive, as

things stand. This is reflected at the top end of profits per the above Table, as the combination of high dividend Income Tax charges and high Corporation Tax rates ultimately bring the net saving to a relative standstill that is slowly eroded once rental profits exceed roughly £130,000 (which is where the lagging corporate/dividend route starts to push the director/shareholder's personal income above £100,000 and the tax-free Personal Allowance is forfeit).

21.2. Comparing Individual Property Investor with a Company (2024/25; differing interest costs)

This second table looks at the potential savings (or costs) to an unincorporated landlord running his or her residential property investment business through a company instead, but this time with different interest cost rates for 2024/25.

	Landlord Comparison: £NILpa Cost of Running Company; Modest Salary with Balance of Profits Taken as Dividends						
	2024/25			2024/25		
Taxable Profit	Net Income as Individual Investor; Interest Cost = 25% of Profit	Net Income Through Company £12.5k* Salary	2024/25 Saving / (Cost) of Incorporation £12.5k* Salary; Interest Cost = 25% of Profit	Net Income as Individual Investor; Interest Cost = 50% of Profit	Net Income Through Company £12.5k* Salary	2024/25 Saving / (Cost) of Incorporation £12.5k* Salary; Interest Cost = 50% of Profit
-	-	-	-	-	-	-
10,000	10,000	9,810	(190)	10,000	9,810	(190)
15,000	14,514	14,054	(460)	14,514	14,054	(460)
20,000	18,514	17,749	(765)	18,514	17,749	(765)
25,000	22,514	21,445	(1,069)	22,514	21,445	(1,069)
30,000	26,514	25,141	(1,373)	26,514	25,141	(1,373)
35,000	30,514	28,836	(1,678)	30,068	28,836	(1,232)
40,000	34,514	32,532	(1,982)	32,568	32,532	(36)
45,000	37,318	36,227	(1,091)	35,068	36,227	1,159
50,000	40,068	39,923	(145)	37,568	39,923	2,355
55,000	42,818	43,619	801	40,068	43,619	3,551
60,000	45,568	47,232	1,664	42,568	47,232	4,664
70,000	51,068	52,252	1,184	46,568	52,252	5,684
80,000	56,568	57,121	553	48,568	57,121	8,553
90,000	59,568	61,990	2,422	52,047	61,990	9,943
100,000	62,568	66,860	4,292	56,297	66,860	10,563
110,000	67,422	71,729	4,307	60,547	71,729	11,182
120,000	72,297	76,598	4,301	64,797	76,598	11,801
130,000	77,172	80,959	3,787	69,047	80,959	11,912
140,000	82,047	84,175	2,128	73,297	84,175	10,878
150,000	86,922	87,391	469	77,547	87,391	9,844
160,000	91,797	90,606	(1,191)	81,797	90,605	8,808
170,000	96,672	94,926	(1,746)	86,047	94,926	8,879
180,000	101,547	99,384	(2,163)	90,297	99,384	9,087
190,000	106,422	103,842	(2,580)	94,547	103,842	9,295
200,000	111,297	108,300	(2,997)	98,797	108,300	9,503
250,000	135,672	130,588	(5,084)	120,047	130,588	10,541
300,000	160,047	153,214	(6,833)	141,297	153,214	11,917

*Salary of £9,000 when profits are only £10,000

Results and Comparisons

1. The table on the **left** assumes that the landlord is paying 1/5th of their income out as residential mortgage interest (e.g., where rental profit after interest is £50,000, the interest cost is 25% of that income – i.e., £12,500, which in turn represents 20% of gross income of £62,500 before interest is deducted. Where rental profit after interest is £200,000, the interest cost is 25% of that income –

Page - 150

i.e., £50,000, which in turn represents 20% of gross income of £250,000 before interest is deducted.

2. The table on the **right** assumes that the landlord is paying 1/3rd of their income out as residential mortgage interest (e.g., where rental profit after interest is £50,000, the interest cost is 50% of that income – i.e., £25,000, which in turn represents 33.3% of gross income of £75,000 before interest is deducted. Where rental profit after interest is £200,000, the interest cost is 50% of that income – i.e., £100,000, which in turn represents 33.3% of gross income of £300,000 before interest is deducted.

The two sets of results demonstrate the importance of the interest charge:

- Where the interest rate is *very* high as in the right-hand table, then the benefit of incorporation is **not** curtailed even by the new higher rates of Corporation Tax, and continues to grow.

- But where the interest rate is comparatively modest as per the left-hand table, the range of profit levels that favour incorporation is significantly narrowed.

- This applies also when comparing those left-hand table results with the 2024/25 results from the previous example at 21.1 (where interest rates fell between the two extremes in the later table above at 21.2).

21.3. Comparing Individual Property Investor with a Company (2015/16 v 2024/25 "No Interest")

This table compares the results for 2015/16, being the final year before dividend taxation was "reformed", with the anticipated results for 2024/25, where the landlord is interest-free.

	2015/16			2024/25		
Taxable Profit	Net Income as Individual Investor; NO INTEREST	Net Income Through Company £8k salary	2015/16 Saving / (Cost) of Incorporation £8k salary; Interest Cost IRRELEVANT	Net Income as Individual Investor; NO INTEREST	Net Income Through Company £12.5k* Salary	2024/25 Saving / (Cost) of Incorporation £12.5k* Salary; NO INTEREST
-	-	-	-	-	-	-
10,000	10,000	9,608	(392)	10,000	9,810	(190)
15,000	14,120	13,608	(512)	14,514	14,054	(460)
20,000	18,120	17,608	(512)	18,514	17,749	(765)
25,000	22,120	21,608	(512)	22,514	21,445	(1,069)
30,000	26,120	25,608	(512)	26,514	25,141	(1,373)
35,000	30,120	29,608	(512)	30,514	28,836	(1,678)
40,000	34,120	33,608	(512)	34,514	32,532	(1,982)
45,000	37,597	37,608	11	38,514	36,227	(2,287)
50,000	40,597	40,944	347	42,514	39,923	(2,591)
55,000	43,597	43,944	347	45,568	43,619	(1,949)
60,000	46,597	46,944	347	48,568	47,232	(1,336)
70,000	52,597	52,944	347	54,568	52,252	(2,316)
80,000	58,597	58,944	347	60,568	57,121	(3,447)
90,000	64,597	64,944	347	66,568	61,990	(4,578)
100,000	70,597	70,944	347	72,568	66,860	(5,708)
110,000	74,597	76,944	2,347	76,568	71,729	(4,839)
120,000	78,597	81,849	3,252	80,568	76,598	(3,970)
130,000	84,357	85,960	1,603	85,297	80,959	(4,338)
140,000	90,357	90,951	594	90,797	84,175	(6,622)
150,000	96,357	96,951	594	96,297	87,391	(8,906)
160,000	101,857	102,951	1,094	101,797	90,606	(11,191)
170,000	107,357	108,850	1,493	107,297	94,926	(12,371)
180,000	112,857	114,406	1,549	112,797	99,384	(13,413)
190,000	118,357	119,962	1,605	118,297	103,842	(14,455)
200,000	123,857	125,517	1,660	123,797	108,300	(15,497)
250,000	151,357	153,295	1,938	151,297	130,588	(20,709)
300,000	178,857	181,073	2,216	178,797	153,214	(25,583)

*salary of £9,000 when profits are £10,000; £12,540 when profits are above £10,000 (2024/5)

The "No interest" comparison assumes that the business has NO finance costs (see Chapter 5) and has to extract all of the company's profits for living expenses, rather than allowing at least some of the funds to "roll up" in the company (see Chapter 4).

The model still assumes a small salary and the rest taken through dividends.

The comparison between 2015/16 and latest reasonable projected outcomes shows the cumulative effects of numerous tax changes over the last several years, such that:

a) In 2015/16, there was very little argument for incorporating a property business or indeed against, not least because the interest relief restriction was not introduced until April 2017.

b) The annual income tax costs in running a property portfolio through a limited company have increased dramatically since then: **purely from an annual incomes tax perspective – and assuming that ALL profits are extracted immediately – it is only when (and for so long as) substantial mortgage interest costs are involved that incorporation may still be attractive**.

c) While interest costs seem likely to rise (or at least stay relatively high) in the near / medium term, mortgages do not tend to last indefinitely and a landlord whose mortgages are approaching term may well decide that the savings offered by operating as a limited company are too transient to merit the upheaval of incorporation, etc. Even so, as we have already discussed, other factors are also relevant to a longer-term assessment of a portfolio and its medium of operation.

21.4. Comparing Net Property Developer (Trading) Income: Personal v Through a Company (2023/24 v 2024/25)

This table looks at the potential savings (or costs) to an unincorporated property developer of running his or her development business through a company instead, comparing 2023/24 with 2024/25.

| | Self-Employed Comparison: £NILpa Cost of Running Company; Modest Salary with Balance of Profits Taken as Dividends ||||||
| | 2023/24 ||| 2024/25 |||
Taxable Profit	Net Income Self Employed	Net Income Through Company £12.5k* Salary	2023/24 Saving/(Cost) of Incorp.	Net Income Self Employed	Net Income Through Company £12.5k* Salary	2024/25 Saving/(Cost) of Incorp.
-	-	-	-	-	-	-
10,000	10,000	9,810	(190)	10,000	9,810	(190)
15,000	14,116	14,097	(19)	14,368	14,054	(314)
20,000	17,666	17,793	127	18,068	17,749	(319)
25,000	21,216	21,489	273	21,768	21,445	(323)
30,000	24,766	25,184	418	25,468	25,141	(327)
35,000	28,316	28,880	564	29,168	28,836	(332)
40,000	31,866	32,576	710	32,868	32,532	(336)
45,000	35,416	36,271	855	36,568	36,227	(341)
50,000	38,966	39,967	1,001	40,268	39,923	(345)
55,000	41,901	43,662	1,761	43,211	43,619	408
60,000	44,801	47,276	2,475	46,111	47,232	1,121
70,000	50,601	52,295	1,694	51,911	52,252	341
80,000	56,401	57,165	764	57,711	57,121	(590)
90,000	62,201	62,034	(167)	63,511	61,990	(1,521)
100,000	68,001	66,903	(1,098)	69,311	66,860	(2,451)
110,000	71,801	71,773	(28)	73,111	71,729	(1,382)
120,000	75,601	76,642	1,041	76,911	76,598	(313)
130,000	80,130	81,003	873	81,440	80,959	(481)
140,000	85,430	84,219	(1,211)	86,740	84,175	(2,565)
150,000	90,730	87,434	(3,296)	92,040	87,391	(4,649)
160,000	96,030	90,650	(5,380)	97,340	90,606	(6,734)
170,000	101,330	94,970	(6,360)	102,640	94,926	(7,714)
180,000	106,630	99,428	(7,202)	107,940	99,384	(8,556)
190,000	111,930	103,886	(8,044)	113,240	103,842	(9,398)
200,000	117,230	108,343	(8,887)	118,540	108,300	(10,240)
250,000	143,730	130,632	(13,098)	145,040	130,588	(14,452)
300,000	170,230	153,258	(16,972)	171,540	153,214	(18,326)

* salary of £9,000 when profits are £10,000

Results and Comparisons

While there remain *some* profit levels at which incorporation is advantageous, these have narrowed markedly from 2023/24 to 2024/25:

1. The most important development when comparing 2024/25 to 2023/24 is that Self-Employed Class 4 NIC rates have fallen significantly in the later tax year:

   2023/24 Main rate of Class 4 NICs between £12,570 and £50,270 = 9%

   2024/25 Main rate of Class 4 NICs between £12,570 and £50,270 = 6%

   In broad terms, staying self-employed no longer costs as much in Class 4 NICs as it used to, making incorporation less attractive than before. The self-employed bill for Class 4 NICs has fallen by as much as £1,131.

2. The "Dividend Allowance" has also fallen from £1,000 to £500, meaning that the dividend route (through incorporation) is typically £44 less efficient.

3. This is on top of the significant increase in company taxation following the re-introduction of a main rate of Corporation Tax of 25%, from April 2023 onwards (that significantly reduced the benefit of incorporation when comparing 2023/24 to 2022/23).

As profits continue to rise in the table, the inherently punitive new Main Rate of Corporation Tax from 2023/24, (the intervening Marginal rate is actually worse), combined with the recently-increased dividend Income tax rates, erodes the early benefits of incorporation to the point where there is a substantial net cost to the corporate route.

To compare:

The marginal tax cost for a self-employed individual once their taxable profits exceed £125,140 since 2023/24 is (45%+2%) = **47.00%.**

In other words, for every additional £1 in taxable profit, they will lose 47pence in taxes.

The marginal tax rate for a singleton director/shareholder whose personal income has exceeded £125,140 since 2023/24 is (100%-(100%-26.5%) x (100%-39.35%)) = **55.42%**

This means that, once business profits have become high enough, the director/shareholder (and their company) will have lost a further 8.42p in combined incomes taxes, for every extra £1 in the company's taxable profits.

That is a very large differential, and is only slightly ameliorated once the new Main Rate of Corporation Tax applies, (as taxable profits exceed £250,000pa), to 54.51%.

Directors of highly-profitable trading companies may well consider that the business would be better off running *un*incorporated – outside of the company.

Unlike with the landlord models above, there is no mitigating variable in terms of residential property finance costs.

Note the assumptions include:

- The model assumes that in the company, the director/shareholder takes a small salary of £12,500, (once profits exceed £10,000 and are able to support such salaries), and then all of the rest of the company's profits as dividends

- The company has already used its Employment Allowance (or is a "singleton" director/shareholder company) so secondary NI Contributions will arise once earnings exceed the Secondary Earnings Threshold, as normal

21.5. Comparing Net Property Developer (Trading) Income: Personal v Through a Company (2015/16 v 2024/25)

It is perhaps worth highlighting the very substantial fall in net income from running a trade or profession through a company, when compared to 2015/16, being the final year before dividend taxation was 'reformed' by the government, and perhaps representing the end of an era spanning many years, in which incorporation had consistently been encouraged by government policy.

	Self-Employed Comparison: £NILpa Cost of Running Company; Modest Salary with Balance of Profits Taken as Dividends						
	2015/16			2024/25		
Taxable Profit	Net Income Self Employed	Net Income Through Company £8k salary	2015/16 Saving / (Cost) of Incorporation	Net Income Self Employed	Net Income Through Company £12.5k* Salary	2024/25 Saving/(Cost) of Incorp.
-	-	-	-	-	-	-
10,000	9,680	9,608	(72)	10,000	9,810	(190)
15,000	13,350	13,608	258	14,368	14,054	(314)
20,000	16,900	17,608	708	18,068	17,749	(319)
25,000	20,450	21,608	1,158	21,768	21,445	(323)
30,000	24,000	25,608	1,608	25,468	25,141	(327)
35,000	27,550	29,608	2,058	29,168	28,836	(332)
40,000	31,100	33,608	2,508	32,868	32,532	(336)
45,000	34,310	37,608	3,298	36,568	36,227	(341)
50,000	37,210	40,944	3,734	40,268	39,923	(345)
55,000	40,110	43,944	3,834	43,211	43,619	408
60,000	43,010	46,944	3,934	46,111	47,232	1,121
70,000	48,810	52,944	4,134	51,911	52,252	341
80,000	54,610	58,944	4,334	57,711	57,121	(590)
90,000	60,410	64,944	4,534	63,511	61,990	(1,521)
100,000	66,210	70,944	4,734	69,311	66,860	(2,451)
110,000	70,010	76,944	6,934	73,111	71,729	(1,382)
120,000	73,810	81,849	8,039	76,911	76,598	(313)
130,000	79,370	85,960	6,590	81,440	80,959	(481)
140,000	85,170	90,951	5,781	86,740	84,175	(2,565)
150,000	90,970	96,951	5,981	92,040	87,391	(4,649)
160,000	96,270	102,951	6,681	97,340	90,606	(6,734)
170,000	101,570	108,850	7,280	102,640	94,926	(7,714)
180,000	106,870	114,406	7,536	107,940	99,384	(8,556)
190,000	112,170	119,962	7,792	113,240	103,842	(9,398)
200,000	117,470	125,517	8,047	118,540	108,300	(10,240)
250,000	143,970	153,295	9,325	145,040	130,588	(14,452)
300,000	170,470	181,073	10,603	171,540	153,214	(18,326)

*2024/25 salary of £9,000 when profits are £10,000; £12,500 when profits are above £10,000

When comparing property investors *without* residential finance costs against property developers, the difference in outcomes is largely attributable to the additional National

Insurance Contributions (NICs) that developers have to pay if they operate in a personal capacity. But even so, the change in tax outcomes for moving to a limited company format, in just a decade, are very significant. Eventually, director/shareholders may come to ask why their net incomes appear to have fallen so much in recent years.

The Government's overall strategy in relation to companies and taxation is not clear-cut. While it does seem clear that the continued fall in tax efficiency for family companies is not accidental, there remain a wide range of company-centric tax incentives, such as:

- Full expensing 100% unlimited relief on capital expenditure on brand-new / unused items of plant and machinery
- Enterprise Investment Scheme (and the 'smaller' Seed Enterprise Investment Scheme) to encourage investment in volatile small companies
- Research and Development expenditure reliefs
- Creative Industry and Cultural tax reliefs – specifically for companies undertaking favoured work on films, animations or video games, theatres, orchestras, etc.
- Corporate Intangibles regime

Milton Keynes UK
Ingram Content Group UK Ltd.
UKHW052307010724
444914UK00001BA/2

9 781739 415372